Storycases

Storycases
Book Surprises to Take Home

RICHARD TABOR

and

SUZANNE RYAN

Illustrated by

Ingrid L. Bowen

1996
TEACHER IDEAS PRESS
A Division of
Libraries Unlimited, Inc.
Englewood, Colorado

TEACHER IDEAS PRESS
A Division of
Libraries Unlimited, Inc.
P.O. Box 6633
Englewood, CO 80155-6633
1-800-237-6124

The following activities are used by permission. Directions for making the Nobody Doll by Patience Brewster Gregg. Printed by permission of the author. Slinky Centipede Memory Game from *Life Cycles Activity Packet*. Copyright 1993 by the Learning Workshop. Reprinted by permission of the publisher.

Production Editor: Heidi Olinger
Typesetting and Design: Kay Minnis
Indexer: Linda Running Bentley

Library of Congress Cataloging-in-Publication Data

Tabor, Richard.
   Storycases : book surprises to take home / Richard Tabor and
Suzanne Ryan ; illustrated by Ingrid L. Bowen.
   xix, 161 p. 22x28 cm.
   Includes bibliographical references and index.
   ISBN 1-56308-199-7
   1. Children's literature--Study and teaching (Early childhood)
2. Children--Books and reading. 3. Early childhood education--
Activity programs. I. Ryan, Suzanne. II. Bowen, Ingrid L.
III. Title.
   LB1139.5.L58T33   1996
   372.64--dc20   96-5020
                                                       CIP

I dedicate this book to all of those individuals, from my childhood to the present, who have encouraged my creativity.

R.C.T.

You may have tangible wealth untold:
Caskets of jewels and coffers of gold.
Richer than I you can never be—
I had a mother who read to me.

from "The Reading Teacher"
by Stickland Gillilan

I dedicate this book to my mother, Marion Brennan.

S.M.R.

Contents

Storycases

Acknowledgments

We wish to thank:

The students and parents of our classes in K.C. Heffernan Elementary School, who enthusiastically responded to our storycases.

Parents and caregivers who took time to do the activities with the children at home and to complete evaluations so that we might further develop the ideas.

The KCH faculty, who showed interest in creating and using the storycases and encouraged us to put the ideas in writing.

The participants in our workshops who were seeking to grow professionally and gain insight into additional ways to provide experiences leading to literacy.

Our illustrator, Ingrid L. Bowen, for her artistic ability to put our ideas and patterns into pictorial form.

Our families who shared us, that we might find time beyond the school day to put our ideas into writing.

Richard's wife, Eunice, for her encouragement, many hours of involvement, and typing the manuscript.

Suzanne's husband, William, for his constant support and willingness to chase down all the loose ends.

Introduction

Storycases provide literacy experiences that children, parents, and peers find enjoyable. This literature connection is in the form of a container, varying from a box or bag to a pet carrier or cookie tin, holding a book or other piece of literature and some related props. Developed for and utilized in primary grade classrooms, storycases have been a successful and popular opportunity for students to have a shared reading experience with family and peers. Storycases lend themselves for use by school and public libraries and are also appropriate for English as a Second Language (ESL) and Chapter I classrooms.

Literacy is promoted when children choose to share books with family and peers through the highly motivational materials of storycases. The use of storycases supports the seven conditions for language learning of researcher Brian Cambourne. Our classroom programs and storycase use incorporate these seven conditions, which include immersing children in written media; demonstrating language use; intentionally engaging children in language experiences; expecting children's accomplishments; responsibility for literature selections by children; allowing children's approximation of the stories; providing opportunities for practice; and response from peers, teachers, and parents. *Storycases: Book Surprises to Take Home* provides examples of storycases that have been successful in the authors' classrooms. The storycase activities herein are designed to be used as presented or as stepping-stones to variations and new possibilities.

Each storycase evolves as a natural extension of a library or classroom literature experience. For example, in sharing *The Enormous Watermelon* (see pages 28–30), puppets are used to depict the story characters. The children in the audience are entranced as the characters come off the printed page and move about, providing a focal point. By using the puppets to tell the story, the storyteller gives the children a model for reading and storytelling. Later, some children will use the book and puppets to approximate the classroom storytelling experience. When not in use, the storycase materials are stored in their container, which is large enough to hold a small version of the book, the puppets, and a note card listing the contents. The children may take the storycases home to share with family and friends. Storycase use fills a need for home-related literature experiences, which current research shows to be essential to successful reading. (See Joyce Epstein. "Theory to Practice: School and Family Partnerships Lead to School Improvement and Student Success." *School, Family and Community Interaction: A View from the Firing Lines.* Ed. Cheryl L. Fagnano and Beverly Z. Werber. Boulder, CO: Westview Press, 1994.)

Use of storycases at home provides parents an opportunity to enjoy literature and its related activities with their children at no expense.

Parent response to the storycases has been positive. One parent has indicated that her son now sees that there is more to books than just reading the words. Parents have offered to create storycases, and our students have collected materials to form their own storycases. Children will be motivated even further by your enthusiasm to explore literature and create related activities.

As shown in the next section, storycases may be prepared with minimal time, materials, skill, and expense. All examples in this text have been successfully used by children in the authors' classrooms and were easily assembled for classroom and library use.

PREPARING STORYCASES

Literature Selection

When selecting literature for storycases, please remember that thousands of children's books are published each year, which provides a wealth of opportunities for storycases. Any book that lends itself to a child-focused activity may be used. So that the expense is minimal, many of our storycases are based on the availability of paperback books. For library use, however, hardback books may be preferred. Since not every book is available in paperback, it is necessary to use some hardbacks to provide quality literature for storycase use.

Following are some questions we ask ourselves or the children when considering books for use in this way. These questions are not given in any particular sequence, nor are they all asked of each book.

- Does the literature lend itself to retelling without exactly quoting the book?
- Does it have distinguishable features, such as easily recognized characters, that may be used in a manipulative form or activity?
- Does it have clearly defined events that may be sequenced or portrayed?
- Would some activity using the events in the book provide skill practice?
- Do the children respond positively to the book and its related activities?
- Do the children indicate a desire to share the book?
- Does the book need something to make it more appealing?
- Will an appealing container help this book circulate by making it more attractive?
- Are there available materials not currently being used, such as a puzzle or game, that might complement this book?
- What will it cost in dollars and time to prepare this storycase?
- How replaceable is the book or accompanying materials if lost or damaged?

Other questions may come to mind as storycase preparations are begun.

Sometimes a storycase just seems to evolve. After hearing a story we have had children say, "that could become a storycase if we put the bear and chicken [referring to the stuffed animals in the classroom] with the book." We also recommend, however, that readers use their discretion to provide books for reading enjoyment on their own without being included in a storycase.

Container Selection

We have used a variety of containers, beginning with readily available, low-cost containers, including old lunch boxes, canvas bags, and boxes. The school and library provided discarded filmstrip cases, game boxes, and outdated reading program containers. As the program grew, adult volunteers began constructing bags from colorful fabric and providing new containers. Garage sales were a source of many inexpensive containers, including briefcases and a variety of bags with pockets and handles. Canvas bags, we discovered, may be labeled and decorated with fabric markers or paint and generally are durable and have sturdy handles.

Below is a list of criteria important to selecting storycase containers.

1. Size
   a. Will all the materials, including the book, easily fit inside? The book should be able to lay flat in the container.
   b. Will it be compact without overcrowding?
   c. Will it store easily when not in circulation?

2. Durability
   a. Will it withstand extended use?
   b. Will it close tightly to prevent the loss of the storycase materials?
   c. Will it withstand varying weather conditions?

3. Appropriateness to the Age Group and Book Contents
   a. Will the container encourage the storycase to be carried home?
   b. Is it appropriate to the age group for which it is intended?
   c. Is it easy to carry or handle?
   d. If the container is to be used in the retelling of the story, is it also functional as a carrier?
   e. Can it be easily labeled?

Following is a list of possible containers.

lunch boxes	shopping bags with handles
briefcases	gym bags
backpacks	suitcases
cookie tins	plastic, reusable storage bags
fabric and vinyl bags	wooden boxes
purses	containers from educational materials
folders with pockets	plastic book bags
pet carriers	camera bags
boxes (e.g., shoeboxes, cereal boxes, game boxes)	expandable envelopes with elastic or Velcro closures

In addition, drawstring bags make an easy-to-close container; the drawstring (a shoelace works well) can be the handle. These bags can be made from attractive print fabric, the size of which will be determined by the contents. A basic size to accommodate many books is 16 1/2 inches long by 10 3/4 inches wide (finished size) with a drawstring casing 3/4 inches deep. Two bags may be made from one-half yard of 44-inch-wide fabric.

MANAGING STORYCASES

Storycases available for circulation may be stored in any area that lends itself to easy access by children. This could be in the book area of the room or on a separate shelf that can accommodate different shapes and sizes of containers. They could also be in an area designated solely for storycases: one teacher stores them in a large laundry basket.

Not all storycases need to be available at the same time. At selected times we have available storycases that complement our current thematic organization, while regularly offering those that children consistently use.

Storycases are designed to be taken home. It is important to include in each case a list of all the components so that borrowers can check contents before returning (see sample labels on page xvii). Before the first storycase is borrowed, a letter is sent to the family explaining what a storycase is. The letter provides information about their use, including the loan policy (see sample letter, fig. I.1, p. xviii).

Storycases may be signed out using the same system for borrowing a library book, that is, by signing the card that goes with it. In our classrooms, each storycase has an index card similar to those used for our regular books, but of a different color for easy identification. The card is removed from the storycase, signed, and placed on a chart that has a pocket for each child. When the storycase is returned, the card is reinserted in the case. Select and use whatever management system fits your classroom or library situation.

Storycases should be evaluated continually. Each of the cases includes a letter reminding the family about storycase use and requesting feedback from the child and parent (see sample letter, fig. I.2, p. xix). As a result of the feedback, the storycase contents or container may be revised. This response will help teachers assess their effectiveness, provide suggestions for additional storycases, and may generate parents' interest in assisting in their preparation. The positive feedback we have received has encouraged us to continue creating and using storycases.

Storycase Labels

The book _____
                                    (book title)
belongs to this storycase.

Other items are:

Thank you for keeping it all together.

                              _____
                                       (teacher's name)

Hi!

I'm a storycase from _____.
                              (enter name of school)

If I'm lost or misplaced please return me.

Thank you.

Dear Family,

Our classroom has been using storycases to help retell stories. Along with a copy of a book or rhyme, the storycase may include props, such as puppets or flannel board figures, a tape recording of the story, or other materials related to the book.

Several of the children have shown an interest in bringing the storycases home. The storycases are to be used by your child to share our classroom literature experiences with family and friends. The class has practiced and talked about appropriate use of the materials. The cases may be borrowed for two days or a weekend, and we ask that your child return each case in the same condition as it went home.

Your child may wish to use any props to aid in telling the story or to act out the story as it is read by another person. The important part of any storycase activity is to share and enjoy literature, which will help develop your child's reading skills.

I hope you and your child will enjoy these storycase experiences.

Sincerely,

Fig. I.1. Letter explaining storycases.

Dear Family,

This is one of the storycases from our classroom. We hope you and your child will have time to enjoy it. The items included may help the book or rhyme to be shared in a way that is comfortable for your child. The main purpose is for you and your child to have a pleasant experience with literature.

Please return the storycase in two days so that others in our class may share this experience with their families. Your comments about using this storycase are appreciated. You may use the form below. Happy storycasing.

Sincerely,

Children should respond to the following questions:

Did you like the storycase?

Was it easy to carry?

Was it easy to use?

Are any pieces missing?

Parents: Please comment on the use of the storycase

_____

(enter book title)

by you and your child, including any suggestions for changes. Thank you.

Fig. I.2. Letter to be included in the storycase container.

Aaron's Shirt

Deborah Gould

New York: Bradbury Press, 1989

SUMMARY

The tee shirt with bold red and white stripes that Aaron chooses when shopping becomes his favorite. He feels that good things happen when he wears the shirt, especially after he wins a teddy bear and makes a new friend during the first two days. Following his mother's idea, he reluctantly puts the shirt in hibernation for the winter. Aaron solves a later problem of outgrowing the shirt by putting it on his bear. This satisfies his mother as well, and he is able to keep his favorite shirt.

ACTIVITY

The child may identify with Aaron's dilemma by dressing and undressing the bear while hearing the story.

MATERIALS

- Copy of book
- Teddy bear
- Red and white tee shirt to fit bear
- Container for all materials, such as a drawstring bag made from a tee shirt. (See instructions on page 2.)

ADDITIONAL NOTES

A journal may go home with this storycase. In it children and parents may write about the experiences the bear had while visiting.

Aaron's Shirt

Directions for making a drawstring bag from a tee shirt

At the bottom of the shirt fold the hem over 1" and stitch, leaving an opening through which to thread a drawstring.

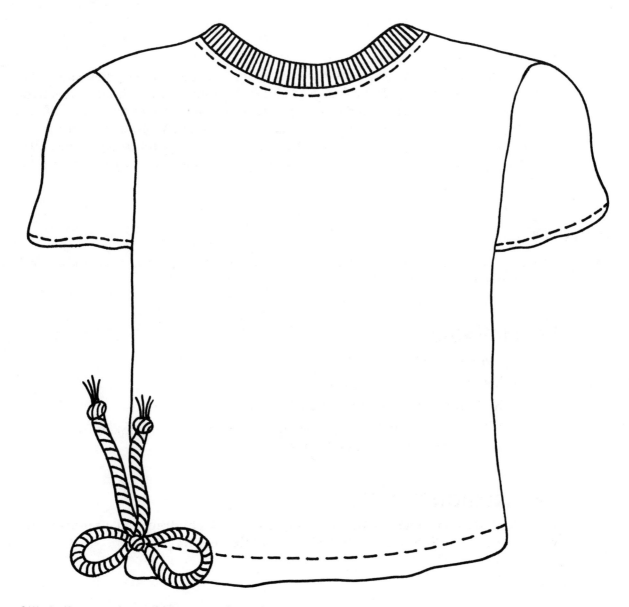

Stitch the neck and sleeves closed.

SUGGESTION: Use a red-and-white striped shirt like Aaron's or a plain white tee shirt and red thread and a red drawstring. Write "Aaron's Shirt" on the bag.

Alphabet Soup

Kate Banks

New York: Alfred A. Knopf, 1988

SUMMARY

An unhappy lunchtime turns into an enjoyable experience. A young boy spells out words with the letters in his soup as the items on the table become objects in a voyage to a fantasy world.

ACTIVITY

Using alphabet pasta or plastic letters, the child can spell out the words illustrated in the story.

MATERIALS

- Copy of book
- Plastic soup bowl
- Plastic spoon
- Alphabet pasta or plastic letters
- Bear-shaped honey container for storing letters
- Container such as a briefcase or wooden wine box with latch. Container needs to protect honey container and bowl from cracking.

Animals Should Definitely Not Act Like People

Judith Barrett
New York: Macmillan, 1988

SUMMARY

For each of the thirteen animals included, the author uses alliteration and illustrations to tell in a humorous way why it is not feasible for animals to participate in the activities of people.

ACTIVITY

Children and parents may compare the student version, *People Should Definitely Not Act Like Animals*, with the original book.

 ## MATERIALS

- Copy of book
- Copy of class or individually created book entitled *People Should Definitely Not Act Like Animals*, based on *Animals Should Definitely Not Act Like People*
- Large envelope to hold both books

The Birthday Thing

SuAnn Kiser and Kevin Kiser

Holmes, PA: The Trumpet Club, 1989

SUMMARY

Using a salt and flour dough he has made, a boy sets out to make a gift for his mother's birthday. He is aided by his brother and creates an unidentifiable object. His father assists him with baking it, and after painting, the item is gift wrapped for his mother. She loves it and finds a special use for her gift.

ACTIVITY

Using project dough (see recipes on pages 6–7), the child, with adult guidance, may make any kind of gift or project.

 ### MATERIALS

- Copy of book
- Laminated recipe card for dough
- Container, such as a reusable storage bag or library bag with hanger

 ### ADDITIONAL NOTES

The recipes may be reproduced for and kept by each child who borrows this storycase.

The Birthday Thing

Recipe card for no-bake project

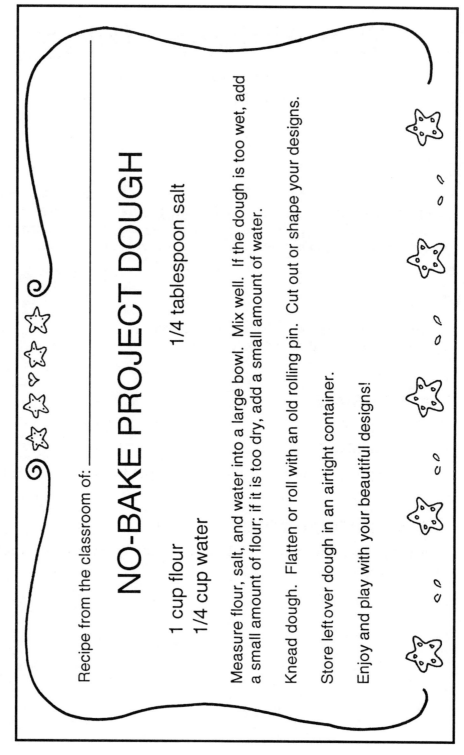

Recipe from the classroom of: _____

NO-BAKE PROJECT DOUGH

1 cup flour   1/4 tablespoon salt
1/4 cup water

Measure flour, salt, and water into a large bowl. Mix well. If the dough is too wet, add a small amount of flour; if it is too dry, add a small amount of water.

Knead dough. Flatten or roll with an old rolling pin. Cut out or shape your designs.

Store leftover dough in an airtight container.

Enjoy and play with your beautiful designs!

From *Storycases: Book Surprises to Take Home.* © 1996. Teacher Ideas Press. 1-800-237-6124.

The Birthday Thing

Recipe card for baked project

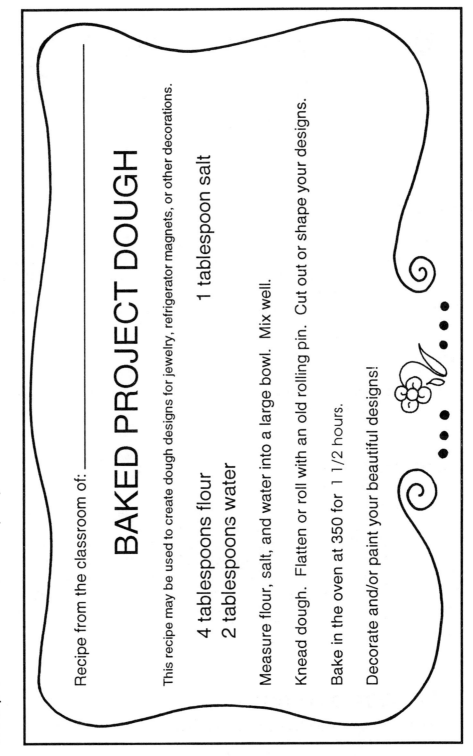

Recipe from the classroom of: _____

BAKED PROJECT DOUGH

This recipe may be used to create dough designs for jewelry, refrigerator magnets, or other decorations.

4 tablespoons flour   1 tablespoon salt
2 tablespoons water

Measure flour, salt, and water into a large bowl. Mix well.

Knead dough. Flatten or roll with an old rolling pin. Cut out or shape your designs.

Bake in the oven at 350 for 1 1/2 hours.

Decorate and/or paint your beautiful designs!

From *Storycases: Book Surprises to Take Home.* © 1996. Teacher Ideas Press. 1-800-237-6124.

Brown Bear, Brown Bear, What Do You See?

Bill Martin, Jr.
New York: Henry Holt, 1992

SUMMARY

Brown Bear is asked the question, "Brown Bear, Brown Bear, what do you see?" In response, he answers, "I see a red bird looking at me." A pattern is established and the question is asked and answered repeatedly throughout the text by different animals. At the conclusion of the book, a mother is asked the question, and her response is, "I see beautiful children looking at me."

ACTIVITY

Child shares class photo album that uses the word pattern from *Brown Bear, Brown Bear, What Do You See?*

MATERIALS

- Copy of book

- Photo album. Prepare or purchase a photo album with enough pages for a picture of each child in the class. You might also have a page for the classroom teacher, class mascot, or other school personnel. Put one photo on each page and text above and below each photo (see example on page 9). The text on the last page with the teacher photo is: "Teacher, teacher, whom do you see?" "I see beautiful children looking at me." If you prepare your own album it is suggested that you laminate and bind the book so it will withstand handling.

- Overnight or duffel bag

ADDITIONAL NOTES

Send a stuffed bear home with the storycase.

Include an instant camera with instructions to take one photo at home (you may ask parents to donate film).

With the stuffed bear may be included a class journal in which children record the bear's visit to their homes.

Brown Bear, Brown Bear, What Do You See?

Sample page from class photo album

I see Kelly looking at me.

Kelly, Kelly, whom do you see?

The Button Box

Margarette S. Reid

New York: Dutton Children's Books, 1990

SUMMARY

In this brightly illustrated book a boy sorts buttons and tells about his experiences with the buttons in Grandma's button box. Information about what buttons are made of is included in the story line, and a postscript explains their origin.

ACTIVITY

The child may sort buttons like the child in the story.

 ### MATERIALS

- Copy of book
- Assortment of buttons in a container, such as a cookie tin
- Canvas bag to transport items

 ### ADDITIONAL NOTES

This storycase is also appropriate for "A Lost Button" in *Frog and Toad Are Friends* by Arnold Lobel (see page 37).

Caps for Sale

Esphyr Slobodkina

New York: HarperCollins Children's Books, 1987

SUMMARY

A cap peddler with all of his caps stacked on his head walks for a long time until he comes to a tree where he sits down to rest. When he wakes up he finds that only one of his caps is left. Monkeys have taken them and mimic the peddler as he scolds them. When he finally throws his remaining cap in frustration, the monkeys do the same, and all the caps are retrieved.

ACTIVITY

Children may use felt figures to illustrate the story as it is read to them or as they retell it themselves.

 ### MATERIALS

- Copy of book
- Large piece of felt for background
- Felt tree (see pattern on page 12)
- Peddler made of felt or paper with felt scrap on reverse
- Set of monkeys
- Set of hats, one for each monkey and the peddler (patterns for the peddler, monkeys, and hats are on page 13)

 ### ADDITIONAL NOTES

Like the peddler, children may practice balancing a stack of real caps on their heads. Include a graph so children may chart the caps they have at home. See page 14 for a reproducible graph.

Caps for Sale

Caps for Sale

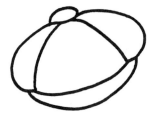 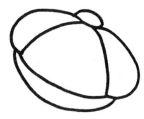

Caps at Our House

Dear Parent,

   After reading *Caps for Sale* with your children, help them inventory the caps at your house by color using the graph below. For each red or blue cap, color in a bar with a red or blue crayon. In the third column (other) fill in the bars with colors matching the other colored or patterned caps your family has. If these caps have patterns you and your child can simply draw and color in the pattern. After the columns have been filled, make a total count of the caps at your house

RED	BLUE	OTHER

TOTAL NUMBER OF CAPS AT YOUR HOUSE

From *Storycases: Book Surprises to Take Home.* © 1996. Teacher Ideas Press. 1-800-237-6124.

Chicka Chicka Boom Boom

Bill Martin, Jr., and John Archambault
New York: Scholastic, 1989

SUMMARY

In this rhythmic alphabet book, the alphabet letters chant their names as they follow each other up a coconut tree. The letters are presented in sequence using uppercase letters in the text and lowercase letters in the illustrations. When the tree is full, it bends and all of the letters fall to the ground in a pile. As they get up, their letter names are used again in sequence.

ACTIVITY

As the story progresses, children place magnetic letters on a cookie sheet, which has a paper tree laminated on it.

 ### MATERIALS

- Copy of book
- Cookie sheet decorated with a coconut tree (see pattern and instructions on page 16)
- Magnetic alphabet letters
- Container for letters such as reusable storage bag
- Drawstring bag to contain all materials

 ### ADDITIONAL NOTES

This activity may be adapted to *The Alphabet Tree* by Leo Lionni (New York: Alfred A. Knopf, 1968).

Chicka Chicka Boom Boom

To make the coconut tree, use no-fade paper and the pattern below

Green leaf: cut 4

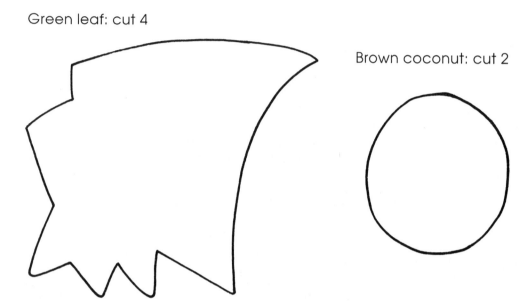

Brown coconut: cut 2

To make the tree trunk, cut a rectangle 1 1/2" wide from light brown construction paper.

Attach the pieces to a cookie sheet with a small amount of rubber cement. Cover the entire surface with clear laminate or vinyl paper. See illustration below for example.

Clifford the Big Red Dog

Norman Bridwell

New York: Scholastic, 1988

SUMMARY

Having the largest dog on the street is fun for his young owner. Although her pet Clifford tries to do the right things, mistakes result because of his size.

ACTIVITY

Using a stuffed red dog, the child play-acts the story as it is read.

 MATERIALS

- Copy of book
- Stuffed red dog
- Cardboard pet carrier, available from a pet store or veterinarian
- Additional props, including leash, dish, and bone
- A journal for recording the events of Clifford's visit

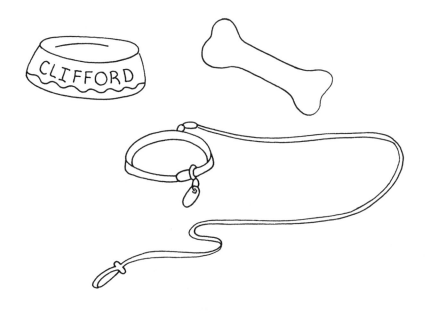

Curious George Goes to the Hospital

Margaret Rey and H. A. Rey

New York: Scholastic, 1973

SUMMARY

After swallowing a piece to a puzzle, Curious George gets a stomachache and has to go to the hospital where he is x-rayed and operated on. He experiences a typical hospital visit, but, as always, has some problems as well.

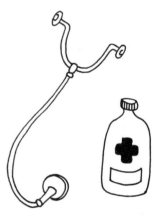

ACTIVITY

The child assembles puzzle that pictures Curious George and play-acts with toy medical items.

 ## MATERIALS

- Copy of book
- Puzzle made by laminating and cutting into interlocking pieces a cover from a paperback edition of the book
- Small box for storing puzzle pieces
- Assortment of toy medical items like those in the story
- Curious George stuffed animal or puppet
- Container such as a canvas or toy medical bag for all materials

ADDITIONAL NOTES

Indicate on the box the number of pieces in the puzzle.

Two puzzles, each with a different number of pieces (e.g., six and twelve), may be included so children may work at their appropriate level.

A puzzle featuring Curious George is recommended, although any approximate puzzle may be included.

The Doorbell Rang

Pat Hutchins

New York: Mulberry, 1989

SUMMARY

Mother gives Sam and Victoria cookies to share. As they begin, the doorbell rings and more children arrive. The cookies are further divided, and more children arrive until there is just one per person. The doorbell rings again, and Grandma arrives with more cookies.

ACTIVITY

Using paper plates and felt or paper cookies, children count out cookies as divided among the children in the story.

MATERIALS

- Copy of book
- Twelve small paper plates
- One larger paper plate or unbreakable tray for cookies
- Twelve felt or paper cookies (see pattern on page 20); dots for chocolate chips may be made with fabric paint or permanent marker
- Container such as a large cookie mix box or cookie tin

ADDITIONAL NOTES

Homemade or store-bought cookies may be used.

The recipe for No-Bake Fudgies on page 20 may be included.

The Doorbell Rang

Recipe card for no-bake fudgies

Recipe from the classroom of:_____

NO BAKE FUDGIES

Mix together in a saucepan:
    2 cups sugar
    1/2 cup cocoa
    1/2 cup margarine (1 stick)
    1/2 cup milk

Bring to a boil. Boil for 3 minutes and remove from the stove.

Add the following and beat until thick:
    1 teaspoon vanilla
    1/2 cup peanut butter
    2 1/2 cups quick oats, uncooked

Drop by teaspoonfuls on waxed paper. Cool before enjoying!

Cut out and laminate recipe card to cardboard. Children who take home this storycase may be given their very own copy of this recipe.

Pattern for felt or paper cookie

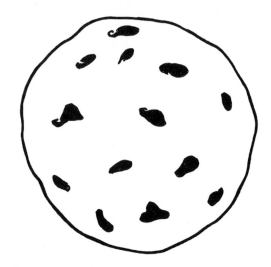

Draw Me a Star

Eric Carle

New York: Philomel, 1992

SUMMARY

In this book, the author-illustrator gives the reader a sampling of his other books as he shows an artist drawing a house, a tree, the sun, a dog, and other animals. In closing he draws the moon and a star on which the artist travels through the night sky. An illustrated page demonstrates how to draw a double star.

ACTIVITY

After reading or listening to a tape recording of the book, the child may practice drawing single stars using the direction card on page 22. For the younger child, a star stencil is provided on page 23.

 MATERIALS

- Copy of book
- Tape recording of the book
- Direction card for drawing stars
- Star stencil
- Star stickers rewarding the child's efforts
- Container, such as an envelope, large enough to hold all materials

 Additional Notes

A page from a calendar featuring Eric Carle may be used to construct the envelope.

Draw Me a Star

Direction card for drawing stars

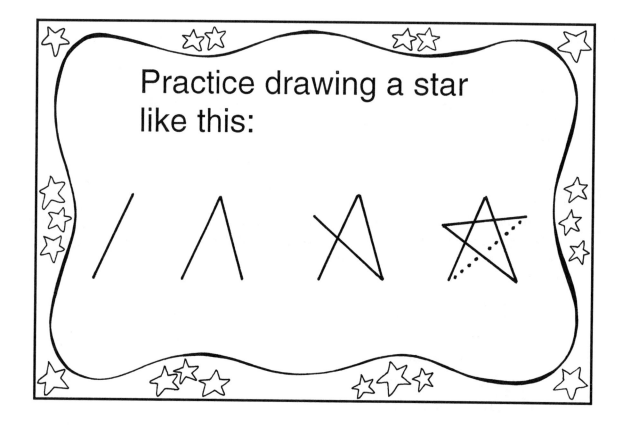

Practice drawing a star like this:

Draw Me a Star

Pattern for star stencil

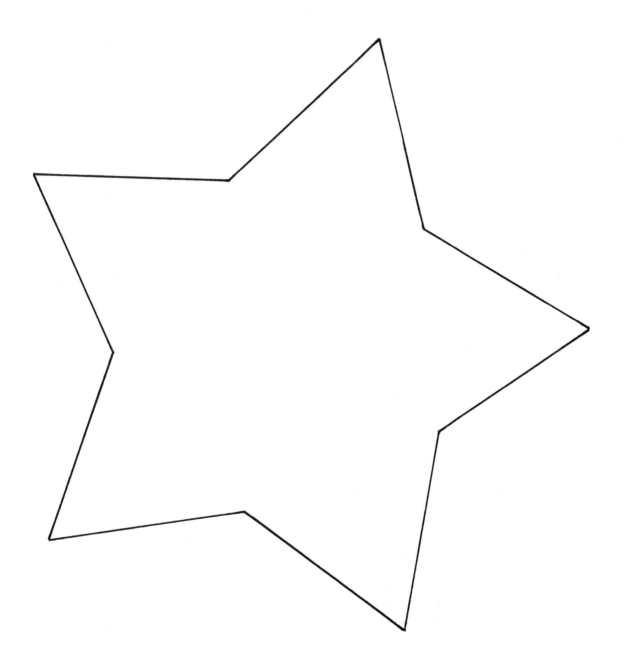

Dreamcatcher

Audrey Osofsky

New York: Orchard, 1992

SUMMARY

The Ojibwa Indians treasured dreams as a source of guidance and wisdom. This book portrays the day of a papoose until naptime when the baby begins to dream. Because the older sister of the infant has woven a dreamcatcher and hung it from the cradleboard, the child is protected from nightmares and surrounded by good dreams. According to legend, the web catches bad dreams and only allows good dreams to filter down to the sleeper and come true.

ACTIVITY

Parent and child work together to construct a dreamcatcher to hang over the child's bed.

 ## MATERIALS

- Copy of book
- Two sets of directions for constructing a dreamcatcher
- Small paper plate
- Ten feet of yarn
- Paper punch
- Expandable envelope with Velcro or an elastic band closure to hold all materials

 ## ADDITIONAL NOTES

Two sets of directions are included for making the dreamcatcher. The first set may be easily completed by a young child. The second set, which is for creating a more authentic dreamcatcher, requires additional materials and adult assistance.

Dreamcatcher

Directions for a paper plate dreamcatcher

1. Use an 8" paper plate. Cut out center of paper plate 1" from edge.

2. Punch holes every 2" around the outside edge of paper plate.

3. Put yarn through one hole and tie a knot.

4. Thread through any hole on the opposite side of the plate.

5. Continue going back and forth across the plate threading the yarn in and out of the holes.

6. A bead may be tied into the center of the weave before the last hole is threaded. Thread the yarn through the last hole, allowing several inches to extend from which to hang the dreamcatcher. Cut off excess yarn.

7. With yarn, tie a feather to the bottom of the dreamcatcher through one of the holes.

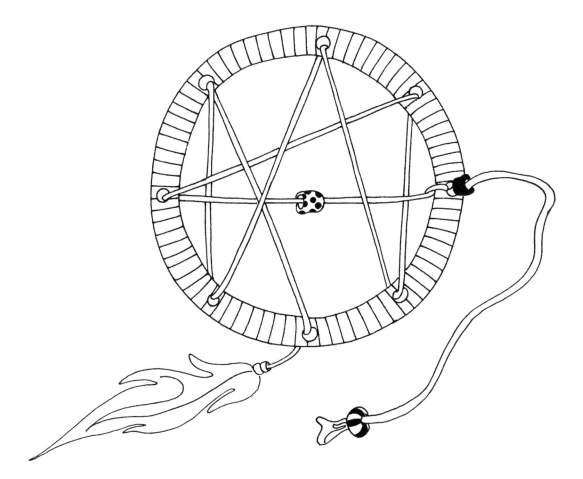

Dreamcatcher

Directions for a traditional dreamcatcher

Materials

a well-soaked willow branch or length of twisted paper
crochet thread, floss, or string
feathers, beads, stones, or shells

1. Form a circle with the branch and tie the ends together, leaving a length of thread from which to hang the dreamcatcher.

2. Cut a piece of crochet thread about 10' long.

3. Make 8 marks on the willow branch equidistant apart. These are the guides for where to tie the thread.

4. Tie one end of the thread on the first mark on the branch. Make a half hitch at a mark on the opposite side of the circle.

5. Continue the same procedure in the middle of each loop. Pull tight.

6. Repeat until you reach the middle of the dreamcatcher.

7. Attach a stone, bead, or shell and tie off the string.

8. Attach a feather to the bottom.

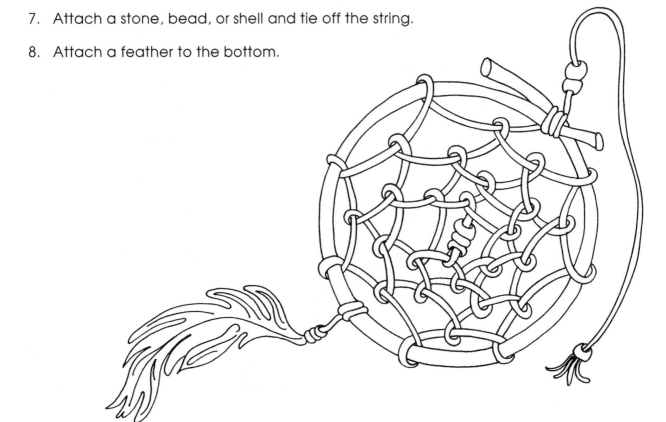

Dreamcatcher

Directions for tying half hitches on the dreamcatchers

Loop the end of the thread around the circled willow branch, having one end longer than the other. Take the short end of the thread and wrap it under and over the long part, pushing the end down through the loop.

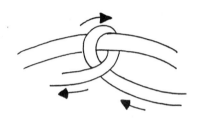

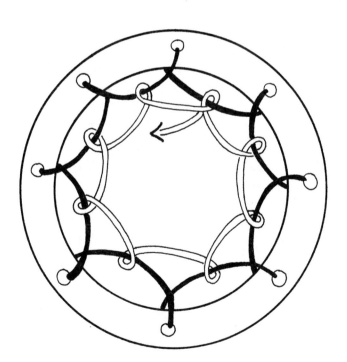

The Enormous Watermelon

Retold by Brenda Parkes and Judith Smith

Crystal Lake, IL: Rigby, 1989

SUMMARY

Mother Hubbard's watermelon grows to be enormous. Nursery rhyme characters Wee Willie Winkie, Jack and Jill, Miss Muffet, and Humpty Dumpty help Mother Hubbard pull up the enormous watermelon. Then they all enjoy eating it.

ACTIVITY

Using glove or finger puppets, participants retell or act out the story as it is read.

MATERIALS

- Copy of book
- Glove or finger puppets (see patterns on pages 29 and 30)
- A plastic lunchbox to contain all materials

ADDITIONAL NOTES

This storycase may be adapted to the *Enormous Turnip*, of which several versions are available.

The Enormous Watermelon

Pattern for the watermelon

Cut watermelon out of green felt and decorate with marker or light green felt.

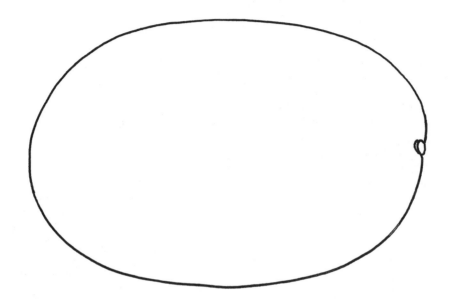

Using a dark brown work glove, attach a piece of Velcro to the palm. If you do not have Velcro simply glue the watermelon to the glove.

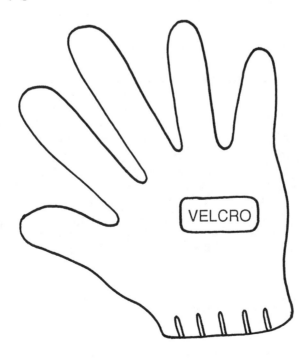

The Enormous Watermelon

Sample of glove or finger puppets for children to use while acting out *The Enormous Watermelon*

Suggestions for creating puppets:
Use yarn and fabric/felt pieces and define the faces with a fabric marker.

WEE WILLIE
WINKIE

JACK AND JILL

MISS
MUFFET

HUMPTY
DUMPTY

OLD MOTHER
HUBBARD

Fast Rolling Fire Trucks

Carolyn Bracken

New York: Putnam Publishing Group, 1984

SUMMARY

This book is a thrill to all young children because it has wheels on the bottom to represent the wheels on a fire truck. The book illustrates the different functions of a fire truck, including the engine, pumper, and ladder truck.

ACTIVITY

After the child has had an opportunity to enjoy the book itself, parents may explain the fire safety tips included in the storycase, which emphasize safe escape routes from the home. Families may practice a fire drill.

 ## MATERIALS

- Copy of book
- Fire safety tips, which may be reproduced from page 32
- Dalmatian figurine
- A drawstring bag to contain all materials

 ## ADDITIONAL NOTES

Any book related to this topic may be included. Suggested titles include *Firehouse Dog* by Amy Hutchings and Richard Hutchings (New York: Scholastic, 1993), *Fire Station* by Robert Munsch (Buffalo, NY: Firefly Books, 1986), and *Matches, Lighters and Firecrackers Are Not Toys* by Dorothy Chlad (Danbury, CT: Childrens, 1982).

Fast Rolling Fire Trucks

Suggested fire safety tips

NEVER PLAY WITH MATCHES OR LIGHTERS

WHEN THERE IS A FIRE, GET OUT FAST

STOP, DROP, AND ROLL IF YOUR CLOTHES CATCH FIRE

CHECK THE BATTERIES ON YOUR SMOKE DETECTOR

KNOW TWO SAFE WAYS OUT OF YOUR HOME

CRAWL LOW IN SMOKE

HAVE FIRE DRILLS AT YOUR HOUSE

ONCE YOU GET OUT, STAY OUT

USE COOL WATER ON BURNS FOR THE BEST FIRST AID

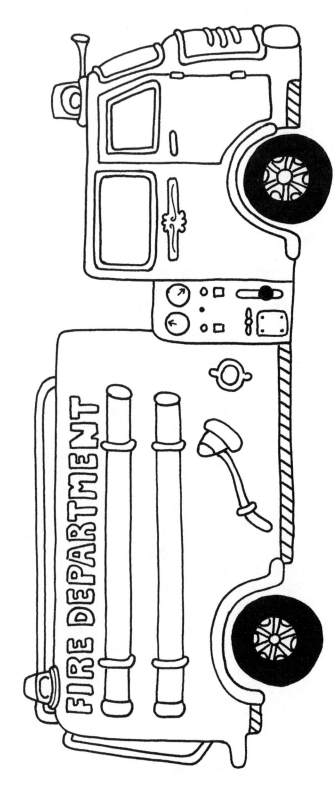

From *Storycases: Book Surprises to Take Home.* © 1996. Teacher Ideas Press. 1-800-237-6124.

Five Little Ducks

Traditional Song
Illustrated by Jose Arrego and Ariane Dewey
New York: Crown, 1989

SUMMARY

Five ducklings wander over the hill away from Mother Duck and manage to lose one sibling at a time. When all the ducklings have disappeared, sad Mother Duck goes out in search of her young and returns with them all.

ACTIVITY

Children start with five ducks and subtract as they listen to the song or story.

MATERIALS

- Copy of book
- Five wooden or paper ducks on popsicle sticks
- One larger or different color duck to represent Mother Duck (see duck patterns on page 34)
- Lunch box to contain all materials

ADDITIONAL NOTES

Story also may be acted out using a metal tray and magnetized ducks (glue magnets to the reverse of the ducks).

Five Little Ducks

Pattern for ducklings

Pattern for Mother Duck

Franklin in the Dark

Paulette Bourgeois
New York: Scholastic, 1990

SUMMARY

Franklin is a young turtle who refuses to go into his dark shell because he is afraid of the dark. He asks several animals for help. In his quest for help, he discovers that the other animals have their own unique fears. Upon returning to his mother, she confesses her own fear that something had happened to him. Franklin overcomes his fear by taking a nightlight into his shell.

ACTIVITY

After reading the book, children and their parents discuss fear. Children then may draw or write about something they are afraid of at night. The writings and drawings will be collected in the class book *I'm Afraid Of*, which accompanies the storycase.*

MATERIALS

- Copy of book
- Flashlight
- Class book, *I'm Afraid Of*, including blank sheets
- Overnight bag to contain all materials

ADDITIONAL NOTES

A nightlight may be included in this storycase.

---

*Teachers and parents should help children choose entries for the class book appropriate for sharing with all classmates and their families.

Franklin in the Dark

Page for class book *I'm Afraid Of*

The teacher should copy this page for each child to complete at home with words, drawings, or both.

At Night I'm Afraid Of

Frog and Toad Are Friends

Arnold Lobel

New York: HarperCollins Children's Books, 1985

SUMMARY

Five short stories in which Toad is awakened in the spring, Toad reads Frog a story, Toad loses a button, Frog and Toad go for a swim, and Toad receives a letter from Frog.

ACTIVITY

The child may match real buttons to those found in "A Lost Button." For "The Letter," the child may read a copy of Frog's letter enclosed in an envelope addressed "A Letter for Toad."

MATERIALS

- Copy of book
- Set of buttons, including 1 black, 1 two-hole, 1 small, 1 square, 1 thin, and 1 white four-hole button that is big, round, and thick
- Reusable storage bag to hold the buttons
- Unsealed envelope addressed "A Letter for Toad"
- Copy of letter in story
- Reversible stick puppet to accompany the stories (see pattern on page 38)
- Large envelope to contain all materials

Frog and Toad Are Friends

Pattern for reversible Frog and Toad stick puppet

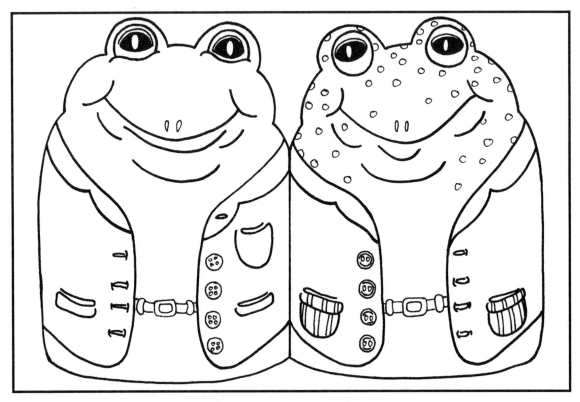

FROG—color green   TOAD—color brown

Note: Differentiate Frog and Toad's clothing with color, pattern, and texture.

Using a 4"-x-6" file card, make a 2-sided Frog and Toad stick puppet. Draw or reproduce the pattern above, crease on the center line, and glue to a wooden craft stick placed between the halves.

Frog and Toad Together

Arnold Lobel

New York: HarperCollins Children's Books, 1972

SUMMARY

Five stories about the experiences of friends Frog and Toad. The two read a book together and Toad makes a list, plants a garden, shares cookies, and has a dream.

ACTIVITY

As the story "A List" is read, the child may cross the events of the story off a list, just as Toad does. In addition, the child may interact with the characters using finger puppets. Finally, the child may use sequence cards to put the events of the book as a whole in order.

MATERIALS

- Copy of book
- Copy of Toad's "A List"
- Pencil
- Finger puppets (see pattern on page 40)
- Sequence cards, created by separating and mounting the pages of a copy of the book
- Cardboard box to contain all materials

ADDITIONAL NOTES

Instructors may choose to include storycase materials for only one of the stories in the series.

Frog and Toad Together

Pattern for finger puppet

Use green or brown felt or construction paper. Add white eyes using a paper punch. Decorate with permanent marker. For a hand puppet, enlarge the pattern to 9" x 12" and fold in half.

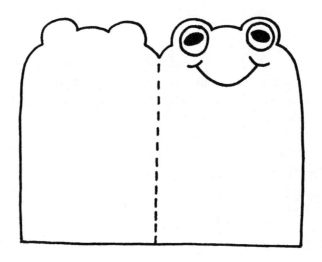

The Gingerbread Boy

Traditional Tale

SUMMARY

After being baked, the gingerbread man escapes from the kitchen and runs away, encountering several people and animals.

ACTIVITY

Children compare different versions of this traditional tale and talk with their parents about how the stories are alike and different. Children and their families may bake gingerbread men.

MATERIALS

- Copies of books listed below
- Gingerbread man cookie cutter
- Copy of the recipe on page 42
- Container for all materials

ADDITIONAL NOTES

Possible versions to use are *Gingerbread Boy* by Paul Galdone (New York: Clarion Books, 1983), *Gingerbread Man* by Eric Kimmel (New York: Holiday House, 1993), *Gingerbread Man,* illustrated by Karen Schmidt (New York: Scholastic, 1985).

The Gingerbread Boy

Recipe card for gingerbread boy cookies

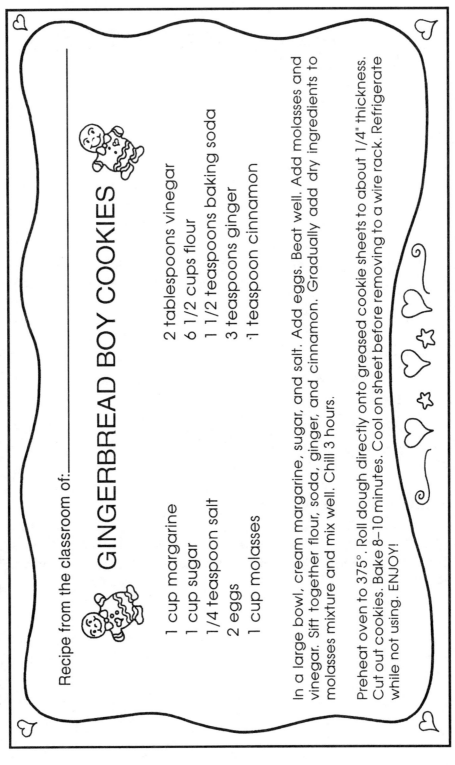

Recipe from the classroom of: _____

GINGERBREAD BOY COOKIES

1 cup margarine
1 cup sugar
1/4 teaspoon salt
2 eggs
1 cup molasses

2 tablespoons vinegar
6 1/2 cups flour
1 1/2 teaspoons baking soda
3 teaspoons ginger
1 teaspoon cinnamon

In a large bowl, cream margarine, sugar, and salt. Add eggs. Beat well. Add molasses and vinegar. Sift together flour, soda, ginger, and cinnamon. Gradually add dry ingredients to molasses mixture and mix well. Chill 3 hours.

Preheat oven to 375°. Roll dough directly onto greased cookie sheets to about 1/4" thickness. Cut out cookies. Bake 8–10 minutes. Cool on sheet before removing to a wire rack. Refrigerate while not using. ENJOY!

Cut out and laminate recipe card to cardboard. Children who take home this storycase may be given their very own copy of this recipe.

From *Storycases: Book Surprises to Take Home.* © 1996. Teacher Ideas Press. 1-800-237-6124.

Good as New!

Barbara Douglas

New York: Lothrop, Lee & Shepard, 1989

SUMMARY

In this story a young child and his grandfather have a bonding experience after a visiting cousin destroys the child's favorite bear. Grandfather comes to the rescue by washing and repairing the bear until he is as good as new.

ACTIVITY

After reading the book with the child, parents may discuss the responsibility of caring for toys. The family may then write about the classroom bear's visit to their home.

 ### MATERIALS

- Copy of book
- Letter of explanation for parents (see reproducible letter on page 44)
- Classroom bear
- Bound book to be used as a journal
- Backpack to contain materials

 ### ADDITIONAL NOTES

The bear may begin to gain personal possessions, such as clothing, as he travels to children's homes.

Good as New!

Dear Parent:

Your child is bringing our classroom bear, Beary Nice, home to visit for the night. After reading and discussing the book *Good as New!* by Barbara Douglas, I would like you to talk with your child about playing responsibly with his or her own and other children's toys. You can then make an entry in Beary Nice's journal about his adventures with your family.

Sincerely,

The Grouchy Ladybug

Eric Carle

New York: HarperCollins Children's Books, 1986

SUMMARY

During each hour of the day, a ladybug encounters increasingly larger animals with which it would like to fight. Thirteen hours later it returns to where it started, on a leaf with a friendly ladybug and some aphids left to eat.

ACTIVITY

Clothespins with pictures of the animals in the story and the hours of the day written on them are attached to a circular board with clock faces indicating the hour. The child is instructed to match the clothespin time and animal to the correct clock from the story.

 ## MATERIALS

- Copy of book
- Twelve-inch corrugated cardboard circle (a cake board may be used)
- Twelve two-inch paper circle clocks (see pattern on page 46) or a small clock stamp
- Fourteen snap-type clothespins
- Copies of animals from story (see reproducible animals on pages 47 and 48)
- Two copies of ladybug, one for the cover of the storycase and one for the circular board (see reproducible ladybug on page 49)
- New, unused pizza box, available from a pizza shop, to contain all items

 ## ADDITIONAL NOTES

To prepare the board, paste or stamp clocks on the outside edge of the cardboard circle. Use a permanent marker to indicate each hour, one through twelve. Color ladybug and attach to the center of the circle.

To prepare clothespins, use a permanent marker to label each one with numerals indicating the hours of the clock with duplicates of 5:00 and 6:00. Color and cut out animals. Using the book as a guide, attach each animal picture to the appropriate clothespin.

Color and attach large ladybug to the top cover of the pizza box. The back of the pizza box may be reinforced with brass fasteners, covered with tape.

The Grouchy Ladybug

To make the board

Use *The Grouchy Ladybug* as a guide. Make 12 clocks using the pattern below. Indicate the hours for 1:00-12:00. Using a 12" cake board or pizza cardboard circle (or make your own), arrange the clocks around the edge, going in the correct time sequence. See illustration below.

Clock pattern

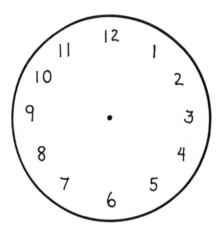

How the board should look

The Grouchy Ladybug

Animal pictures

Copy and color the animal pictures. Cut out and fasten each animal box to a snap-type clothespin. Write the time indicated in the book (e.g., 7:00) on the clothespin adjacent to the appropriate picture.

The Grouchy Ladybug

Animal pictures

The Grouchy Ladybug

Ladybug pattern

Pattern for ladybug to be used on the cover of the storycase as well as in the center of the board. Make two copies of the ladybug, cut out, and color.

Group Soup

Barbara Brenner

New York: Penguin Books, 1992

SUMMARY

Six hungry rabbit children head home, only to discover that they must prepare their own dinner. Four of them assist brother Ricky by providing the ingredients for soup. Cranky Rhoda does not want to help, but when she finally provides the missing ingredient, everyone is pleased with the resulting group soup. This book naturally brings out the importance of collaboration.

ACTIVITY

Using make-believe ingredients, children may sequentially contribute the items as the group soup is created in the story.

MATERIALS

- Copy of book
- Paper soup ingredients made from the patterns on pages 51–52
- Reusable storage bag to contain all items

ADDITIONAL NOTES

This book lends itself to a project of making real soup.

Group Soup

To make the pot and the water

The pot is made from a 10" circle of gray paper.

The water is made from a 9 1/2" circle of clear laminate or vinyl.

Patterns for soup ingredients

Cut from heavy colored paper, decorate, label, and laminate.

Group Soup

Patterns for soup ingredients

Cut from heavy colored paper, decorate, label, and laminate.

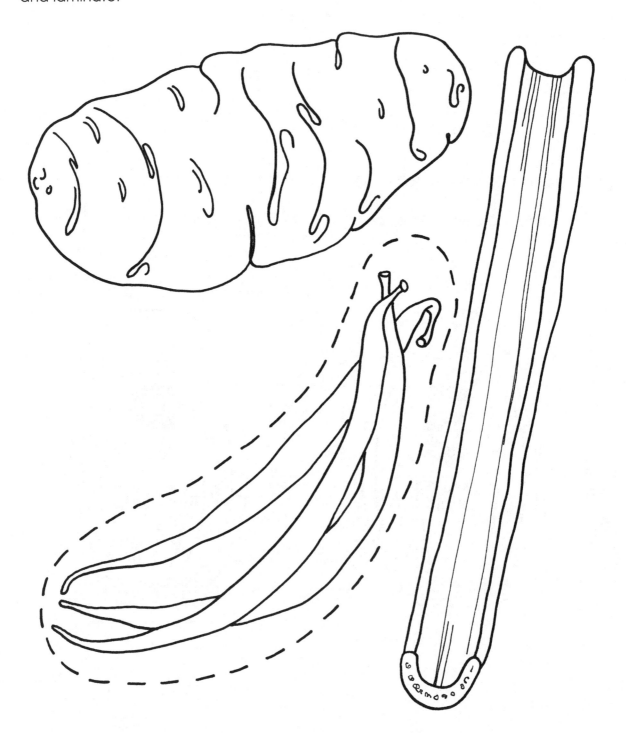

Group Soup

Patterns for soup ingredients

Cut from heavy colored paper, decorate, label, and laminate.

How Many Bugs in a Box?

David A. Carter

New York: Simon & Schuster, 1988

SUMMARY

In this pop-up book children are introduced to the number concepts one through ten, color words, shapes, and sizes. Each box in the book pops open to reveal a different number and species of bug.

ACTIVITY

The child first may read the book for enjoyment and then read it a second time to count the bugs in each box. The child is then provided with a collection of bugs with which to practice counting.

 ## MATERIALS

- Copy of book
- Collection of plastic bugs
- Box to hold bugs
- Drawstring bag with a bug print to contain all materials

 ## ADDITIONAL NOTES

The book and tape *We Like Bugs* by Joelene Griffith (East Wenatchee, WA: Learning Workshop, 1993) may be used with this storycase. *Bugs* by Nancy Winslow Parker and Joan Richards Wright (New York: Scholastic, 1987) contains educational information about bugs.

Children may create their own bug puzzle by aligning and taping together six craft sticks. Draw a bug on the reverse of the sticks, remove the tape and mix up the sticks. The child now has a puzzle to reassemble.

I Know an Old Lady
Who Swallowed a Fly

Gail Gibbons
New York: Holiday House, 1991

SUMMARY

In this familiar tale, an old lady swallows a fly and continues to swallow larger and larger animals until she dies. Children enjoy the nonsense of an old lady swallowing a goat, a cow, a horse, and so on.

ACTIVITY

As the story is read to the child, the child drops animals into a plastic bag attached to the back of a cardboard figure of the old lady.

 ### MATERIALS

- Copy of book
- Cardboard doll of the old lady dressed with scrap fabrics (see pattern on page 56)
- Animals made from cardboard or oak tag (see patterns on pages 57–59)
- Reusable storage bag to hold animals
- An old purse to contain all materials

 ### ADDITIONAL NOTES

Another version of this tale is *I Know an Old Lady Who Swallowed a Fly*, adapted and illustrated by Colin Hawkins and Jacqui Hawkins (New York: Putnam Publishing Group, 1987).

I Know an Old Lady Who Swallowed a Fly

Pattern for the Old Lady

Enlarge pattern, cut from cardboard, and attach a plastic bag to the reverse.

I Know an Old Lady
Who Swallowed a Fly

Patterns for animals

Cut from cardboard. Size of animals should follow the size of the animals in the story.

I Know an Old Lady
Who Swallowed a Fly

Patterns for animals

Cut from cardboard. Size of animals should follow the size of the animals in the story.

I Know an Old Lady
Who Swallowed a Fly

Patterns for animals

Cut from cardboard. Size of animals should follow the size of the animals in the story.

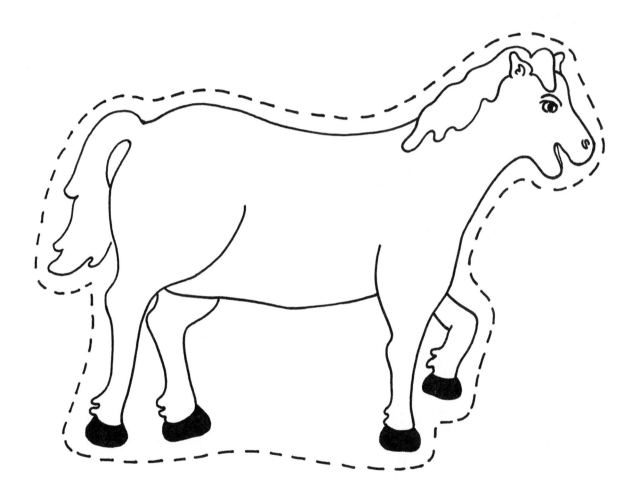

If You Give a
Mouse a Cookie
Laura Joffe Numeroff
New York: Scholastic, 1985

SUMMARY

This is a circle story in which a young boy offers a mouse a cookie. His offer has a domino effect that leads to a glass of milk, drawing a picture, and eventually another glass of milk.

ACTIVITY

The child arranges pictures of the items in the story sequentially according to the events that take place.

MATERIALS

- Copy of book
- Pictures of the items from the story (see reproducible items on page 62)
- Set of make-believe cookies (see pattern on page 61)
- Grocery bag or brown Kraft paper for making container to hold all materials (see directions on page 63)

ADDITIONAL NOTES

A collection of small items from the story may be included in the storycase. This storycase also may be adapted to *If You Give a Moose a Muffin* by Laura Numeroff (New York: HarperCollins Children's Books, 1994).

If You Give a Mouse a Cookie

Cookie pattern

Cut 15 cookies from a brown grocery bag or brown Kraft paper. Cut out the illustrations on page 62 and glue one picture to each of the 15 cookies. Laminate each cookie.

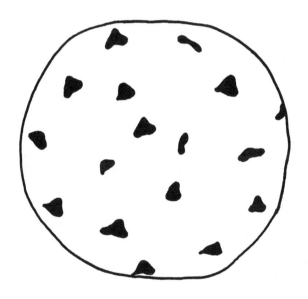

If You Give a Mouse a Cookie

Illustrations from the story

Cut out the pictures below and glue one picture to each of the 15 cookies.

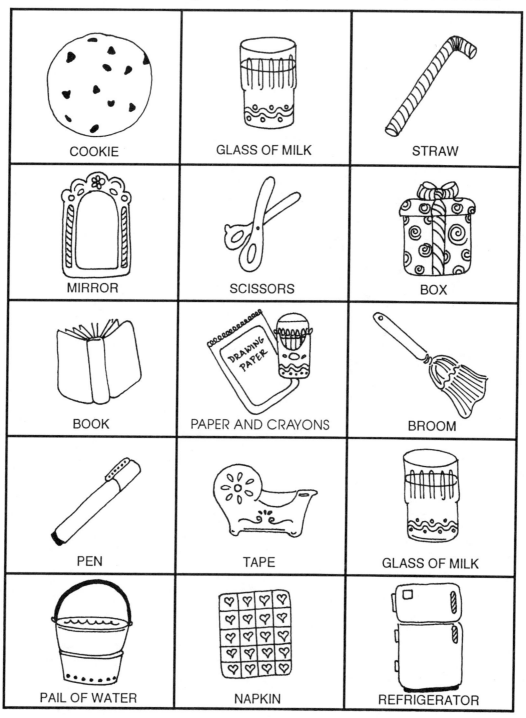

If You Give a Mouse a Cookie

Directions for making the storycase container

Materials

Large brown grocery bag, glue, stapler, wide clear tape.

To make the storycase

Cut open grocery bag so that it will lie flat by cutting along the glued seam and around four sides of the base.

Cut off glued seam and set aside to be used as a handle.

Fold one side over 12" and cut off excess. Ensure any printing is on the inside.

Cut a partial circle from fold, leaving a 9" flat base at fold. See illustration below:

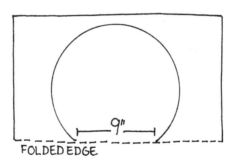

FOLDED EDGE

Reinforce edges with clear tape.

Label with book title and draw on chocolate chips.

Cover the entire bag with clear plastic. Cover handle with plastic and attach to the top opening with staples or heavy tape.

Jack and the Beanstalk

Retold by John Howe
Boston: Little, Brown, 1989

SUMMARY

In this traditional tale, magic beans grow into a huge beanstalk. The boy, Jack, curious to find out where it goes, starts climbing and finds himself at the home of a giant. Jack escapes with a hen that lays golden eggs, a bag of coins, and a harp. Later the giant is killed when Jack cuts the beanstalk down.

ACTIVITY

Children match corresponding lower- and uppercase letters using gold paper eggs, coins, and beans.

 ### MATERIALS

- Copy of book
- Set of lowercase alphabet letters on golden "eggs"
- Set of uppercase alphabet letters on gold "coins" (patterns for the coins and eggs are on page 65)
- Egg-shaped instruction card (see pattern on page 65)
- Reusable storage bag or plastic egg sprayed gold
- Storycase container

 ### ADDITIONAL NOTES

Lima beans, sprayed gold, and green paper or artificial leaves also may be used for letters.

Jack and the Beanstalk

Instruction card

To be cut out.

Match the
<u>lowercase</u> letters
on the golden eggs with
the <u>CAPITAL</u> letters on the
golden coins.

Golden egg pattern

Gold coin pattern

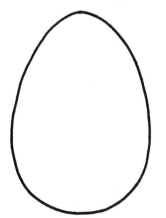

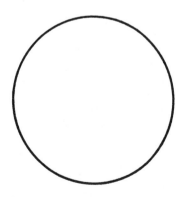

Cut eggs and coins out of gold paper
or tag board. White tag board may
be sprayed gold.

Jesse Bear, What Will You Wear?

Nancy Carlstrom
New York: Macmillan, 1986

SUMMARY

This book relates a day in the life of a young bear. Jesse Bear not only wears different items of clothing, but also wears food in his hair, among other things with which young children may identify.

ACTIVITY

Children practice color word recognition by selecting cards that designate the colors of clothing in which to dress Jesse Bear.

MATERIALS

- Copy of book
- Fake fur or construction paper bear (see pattern on page 67)
- Shirts and pants made from varying colors of felt or construction paper (see patterns on page 68)
- Pants- and shirt-shaped color word cards to match the clothing colors (patterns and instructions are on page 69)
- Instruction card (see reproducible example on page 69)
- Cue cards showing actual colors and their word designations
- Reusable storage bag to hold cards
- Reusable storage bag to hold clothes
- Expansion folder to hold all materials

ADDITIONAL NOTES

This storycase is an appropriate accompaniment to "What Will Little Bear Wear?" from *Little Bear* by Else Holmelund Minarik (New York: Harper & Row, 1957).

Jesse Bear, What Will You Wear?

Pattern for Jesse Bear

Jesse Bear, What Will You Wear?

Clothing patterns for Jesse Bear

Cut patterns from either felt or colored paper.

Shirt pattern

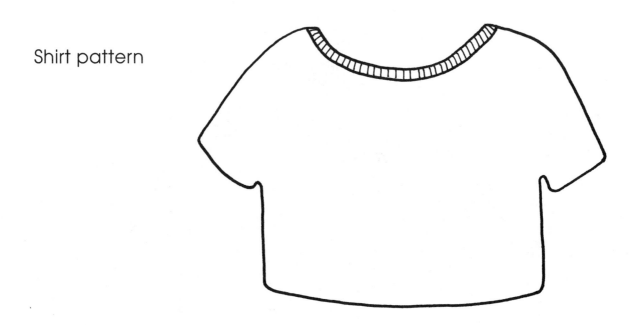

Pants pattern

Jesse Bear, What Will You Wear?

Directions for making color word cards

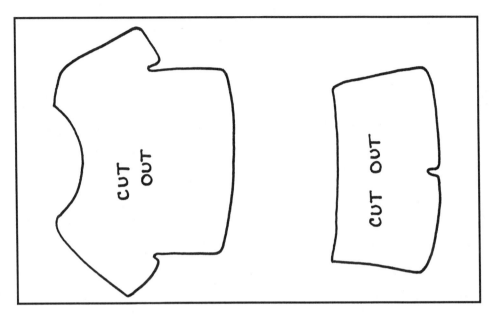

Using a 3"-x-5" card and the patterns above, cut out shirts and pants. Write "shirt" or "pants," as appropriate, on one side of each shape. Write a color word on the reverse of each shape.

Instruction card for dressing <u>Jesse Bear</u>

> ### *Jesse Bear, What Will You Wear?*
>
> Make a pile of shirt cards.
>
> Make a pile of pants cards.
>
> Take one card from each pile.
>
> Read the color word.
>
> If you don't know the color word, look on the cue card, matching the color to its word designation.
>
> Dress Jesse Bear with the colors indicated on the cards.

From *Storycases: Book Surprises to Take Home.* © 1996. Teacher Ideas Press. 1-800-237-6124.

Jump, Frog, Jump!

Robert Kalan

New York: Scholastic, 1981

SUMMARY

This text uses repetitive phrases to tell the story of a frog who escapes a variety of situations encountered in his natural environment.

ACTIVITY

According to the sequence of events in the book, a frog is moved around a game board that pictures objects from the story.

MATERIALS

- Copy of book
- Game board made from posterboard and featuring objects from the story (see patterns on pages 71–73)
- Plastic or card stock frog (see pattern on page 74)
- Box, such as a used game box, to contain all materials

ADDITIONAL NOTES

A related book is *Jog, Frog, Jog* by Barbara Gregorich (Grand Haven, MI: School Zone, 1992).

Jump, Frog, Jump!

Patterns and directions for the *Jump, Frog, Jump!* game board

Cut blue posterboard to 16" square and fold in half so that it will fit into a game board box. Reproduce and color or decorate figures pictured below and on pages 72–73. Cut out and glue the figures to the game board. Cover the finished product with a clear, protective covering. A discarded game board may be substituted for the posterboard.

Patterns for the figures

Jump, Frog, Jump!

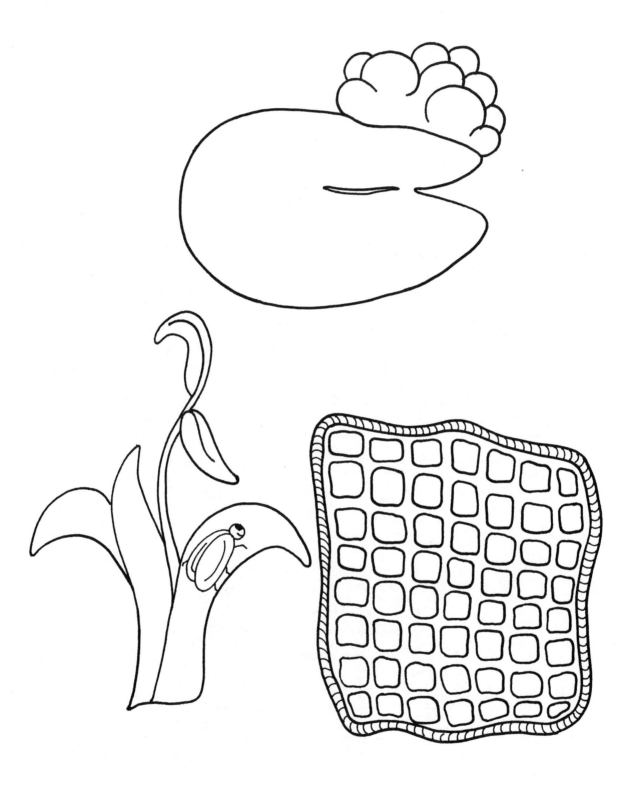

Jump, Frog, Jump!

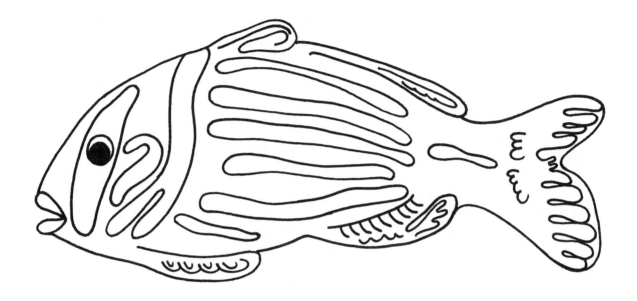

Jump, Frog, Jump!

Pattern for jumping frog to be moved around the game board

Trace frog pattern onto a 3"-x-5" index card, cut out, and fold on the dotted line. Color and decorate.

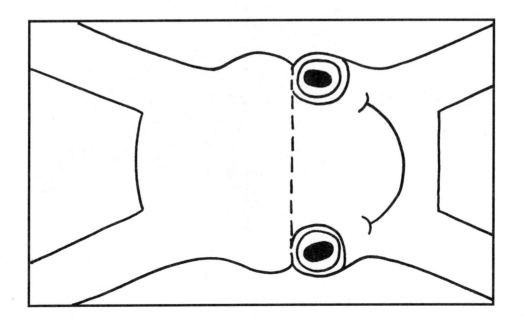

Lace Them Up

Patricia Quinlan and Lily Barnes
New York: Hyperion Books, 1992

SUMMARY

This is the story of a young child's first pair of tie shoes. With a little help and a considerable amount of practice, Lisa finally masters the task. The book includes a shoe card and laces.

ACTIVITY

After reading the book with the child, parents may lend help in learning to tie. The child then may practice. Families also may enjoy making a shoe card to practice with at home.

MATERIALS

- Copy of book
- Shoe card and laces (see directions on page 76)
- Shoebox, the lid of which serves as a shoe card, to contain all materials

ADDITIONAL NOTES

Other materials that will afford practice in tying may be included.

Two related books are *The Shoelace Book* by Golden Books, New York, and *All by Myself* by Mercer Mayer (New York: Golden Books, 1985).

Lace Them Up

Directions for making a shoe card

Punch holes into and decorate the card to look like a shoe. Lace a shoestring through the holes and tie.

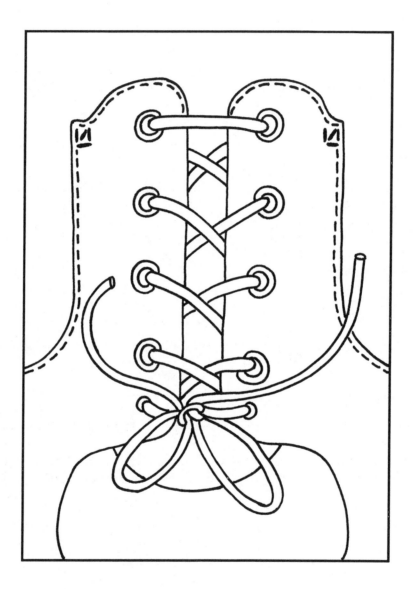

Suggestion: Make a shoe card out of the lid of the shoebox used as the storycase container.

The Little Engine That Could
Retold by Watty Piper
New York: Putnam Publishing Group, 1991

and

Freight Train
Donald Crews
New York: Greenwillow Books, 1978

SUMMARIES

In *The Little Engine That Could*, a small engine, by believing in himself and repeating the phrase, "I think I can, I think I can," is able to accomplish a task that the larger, newer trains are unable to do.

Freight Train briefly traces the journey of a colorful train as it goes through tunnels, by cities, and over trestles.

ACTIVITY

The child plays with a toy train while listening to the stories along with other family members. Parents then help their child graph their favorite book and the favorite book of other family members and friends.

MATERIALS

- Copies of both books
- Toy train
- Booklet for graphing (see reproducible graph on page 78)
- Letter to parents about graphing (see sample letter on page 79)
- Storycase container, the outside of which may be decorated with railroad designs

ADDITIONAL NOTES

Toy trains may be purchased from T. C. Timber; train cases are available from Mattel.

The Little Engine That Could

The book _____'s family and friends
liked best:

The Little Engine That Could	*Freight Train*

The Little Engine That Could

Letter to parents

Dear Family,

During this school year we have been learning about graphs. This storycase includes a graph that your child can do at home. After sharing the two books with family members, your child may chart the book each person liked best. On a new sheet in the graph booklet enclosed, your child may record each person's choice by coloring in a box above the title of the book chosen. This graph may be shared in class when the storycase is returned. Thank you for contributing to a learning experience.

Sincerely,

From *Storycases: Book Surprises to Take Home.* © 1996. Teacher Ideas Press. 1-800-237-6124.

Little Miss Muffet
Traditional Rhyme

Little Miss Muffet

Little Miss Muffet
Sat on a tuffet
Eating her curds and whey.
Along came a spider
Who sat down beside her
And frightened Miss Muffet away.

ACTIVITY

The child may act out the rhyme at home with one other person. One person portrays Miss Muffet, and the other plays the part of the spider as the poem is read to or with the child.

✏ MATERIALS

- Copy of rhyme on a laminated card
- Bowl
- Spoon
- Toy spider with string attached
- Plastic bowl with a snap-on lid to contain all materials

Little Red Hen

Paul Galdone
Boston: Clarion Books, 1985

SUMMARY

In this traditional tale, the Little Red Hen finds that her animal friends are reluctant to help her plant, harvest, and grind wheat into flour. After she has used the flour to make bread, the animals want to join her in eating it, but she refuses.

ACTIVITY

Hand puppets are used by the child as the story is read or retold.

 ### MATERIALS

- Copy of book
- Hand puppet of hen (see pattern on page 82)
- Glove puppet of other animal characters in story (see pattern on page 83). When using another version of this tale, ensure the puppet characters correspond.
- Bread bag to contain all materials

 ### ADDITIONAL NOTES

More information on bread is available in *Bread, Bread, Bread* by Ann Morris (New York: Scholastic, 1989).

The recipe for Simple Bread on page 84 may also be included.

Little Red Hen

Pattern for Little Red Hen hand puppet

Cut out pattern and place long edge on fold of fabric. Pin in place and cut 2 "hens," as indicated by the solid black line. Remove pattern, unfold fabric, and pin halves together. Stitch halves together 1/4" from edge of fabric, as indicated by the dotted line.

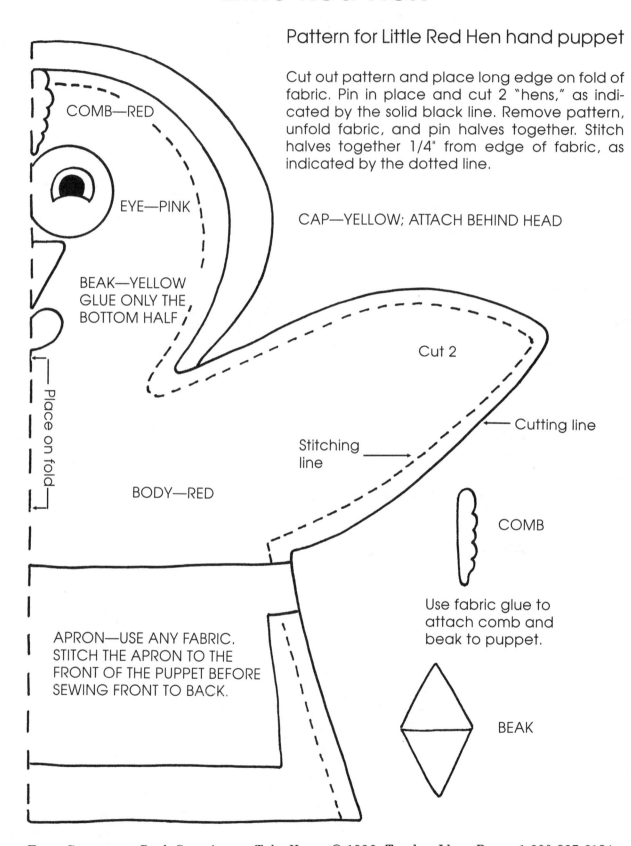

COMB—RED

EYE—PINK

CAP—YELLOW; ATTACH BEHIND HEAD

BEAK—YELLOW
GLUE ONLY THE
BOTTOM HALF

Place on fold

BODY—RED

Cut 2

Stitching line

Cutting line

COMB

Use fabric glue to attach comb and beak to puppet.

APRON—USE ANY FABRIC.
STITCH THE APRON TO THE
FRONT OF THE PUPPET BEFORE
SEWING FRONT TO BACK.

BEAK

Little Red Hen

Pattern for animal glove puppet

Using the patterns below, cut the animals from felt. Attach the shapes to a work glove and add facial features with a marker.

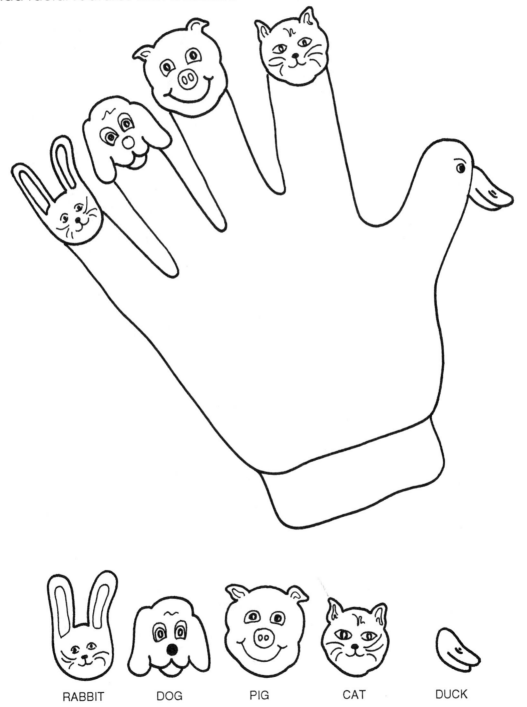

RABBIT   DOG   PIG   CAT   DUCK

Little Red Hen

Recipe card for simple bread

Recipe from the classroom of: _____

SIMPLE BREAD

2 1/2 cups warm water
1 tablespoon salt
2/3 cups milk
1/3 cup cooking oil

2 packages active dry yeast
7 to 7 1/2 cups flour
2 tablespoons sugar

Measure water and yeast into mixing bowl. Stir until well blended and allow to stand for 10 minutes. Add milk, sugar, salt, oil, and about half of the flour. Blend well and beat until smooth. Add enough flour to make a soft dough. Knead on floured surface until smooth. Shape into two loaves and place into two well-greased bread pans. Cover, place in a warm, draft-free area, and allow to rise until double in bulk, about 2 hours. Bake at 375° for 35 to 40 minutes. Bread is done when nicely browned and when top is tapped, it sounds hollow. Remove from pans and cool on rack. Allow to cool thoroughly before slicing.

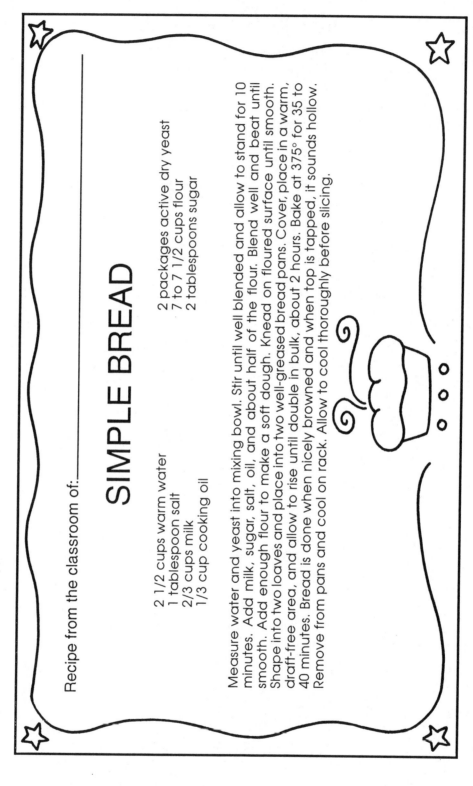

Cut out and laminate recipe card to cardboard. Children who take home this storycase may be given their very own copy of this recipe.

From *Storycases: Book Surprises to Take Home.* © 1996. Teacher Ideas Press. 1-800-237-6124.

Mouse Count

Ellen Stoll Walsh

New York: Harcourt Brace Jovanovich, 1991

SUMMARY

Ten mice meet near-disaster as a snake gathers them for dinner. The snake spies three mice and places them in a jar. Three is not enough so he continues until he has ten, counting as he places them in the jar. The mice trick him into pursuing a larger mouse, which is actually a gray rock, and while he's away, they escape from the jar, counting as they go.

ACTIVITY

Using a sock snake puppet, the child counts make-believe mice into a jar and then removes them to a flannel board as the story progresses.

MATERIALS

- Copy of book
- Snake puppet made from a sock
- Ten felt or fabric mice (see pattern on page 86)
- Plastic jar with lid
- Felt or fabric rock (see pattern on page 86)
- Felt for a flannel board
- Shopping bag to contain all materials

ADDITIONAL NOTES

This storycase may be adapted to *Ten Little Mice* by Joyce Dunbar (Orlando, FL: Harcourt Brace, 1992).

Mouse Count

Pattern for fabric mice

Cut 10 from brown felt. Ears may be made of a contrasting color and glued on.

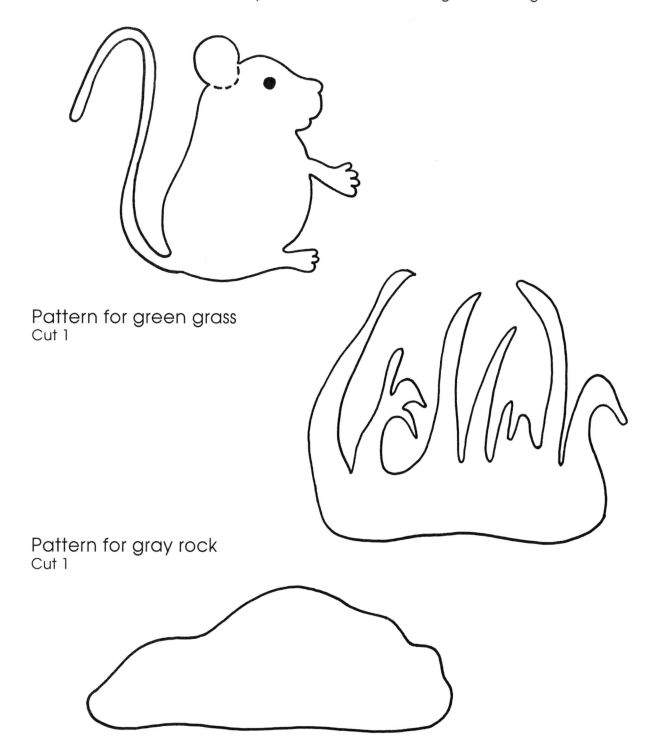

Pattern for green grass
Cut 1

Pattern for gray rock
Cut 1

Mousekin's Golden House

Edna Miller

New York: Simon & Schuster, 1964

SUMMARY

A whitefoot mouse comes upon a discarded jack-o'-lantern, which he uses for safety from a cat and other predators. As the weather gets colder, he fills it with milkweed down. The carved face closes up as the jack-o'-lantern shrinks, becoming Mousekin's winter home.

ACTIVITY

The child manipulates the finger puppet mouse while reading the story.

 ### MATERIALS

- Copy of book
- Mouse finger puppet (see pattern and directions on page 88)
- Jack-o'-lantern sack to contain all materials (see pattern and directions on page 89)

 ### ADDITIONAL NOTES

A plastic jack-o'-lantern bucket or bag also may be used for the storycase container.

Mousekin's Golden House

Pattern for Mousekin finger puppet

Using the pattern below, cut 2 "mice" from felt or other fabric. Glue the edges, leaving an opening at the bottom. Attach ears, tail, and feet with glue, as indicated.

Mousekin's Golden House

Pattern for jack-o'-lantern bag

Enlarge pattern to 8 1/2"-x-11". Cut out the pattern and place the straight edge on the fold of the fabric. (Polyester is recommended.) Pin in place.

Cut out 2 pumpkins with eyes, mouth, and nose. These will make the front and back of the bag.

Cut out 2 pumpkins without any openings. These will make the inside lining of the bag.

Cut 2 pumpkins out of batting without openings. These will make the inside lining of the bag.

Cut 2 pumpkins out of batting without openings. Pin the batting to the wrong side of the outside pieces. Pin right sides of outside pieces and lining together. Stitch rounded sides of pumpkin, leaving top open. Clip rounded edges and press seams open. Turn right sides out. Finish the top opening with a whip or hem stitch. Secure the batting by topstitching vertical lines like those on an actual pumpkin rind (see illustration at bottom right).

Sew the front and back of the bag together. Stitch a handle, cut from green or black fabric, to the inside edge of the bag.

Nobody

Patience Brewster

New York: Clarion Books, 1982

SUMMARY

A child returns from a day in school, exhausted and out of sorts. Her mother questions and attempts to cheer her up with typical questions such as "Who passed out the snack today?" and "Who cleaned up the toys?" The child continually responds with "nobody," and Nobody is born in the imaginations of both mother and child. Nobody becomes a constant, imaginary companion until the child's birthday when she receives a Nobody doll as a gift.

ACTIVITY

As the book is read, the child can use a Nobody doll to act out the parts on the page.

 MATERIALS

- Copy of book
- Nobody doll (see pattern and instructions on pages 91–93)
- Gift box with a bow on top to contain all materials

Nobody

Pattern for Nobody doll

Nobody's head and body: cut 2

Nobody

Pattern for Nobody doll

Nobody's arms: cut 2

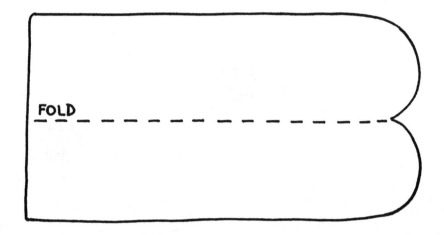

FOLD

Nobody's ears: cut 4

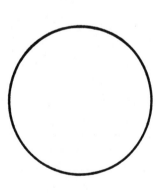

Nobody's feet: cut 4

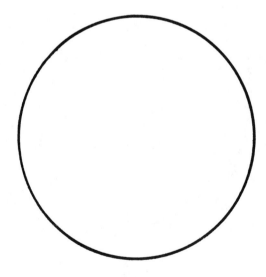

Nobody

Directions for making the Nobody doll

Materials

    1/4 yard unbleached muslin
    cotton batting
    black thread, embroidery floss, or fabric marker
    quilting thread

Instructions

1. Cut pattern pieces from muslin.

2. Using the illustrations in *Nobody* as a guide, add facial features with a black fabric marker, thread, or embroidery floss.

3. With right sides together, stitch the head and body together leaving a 2" opening at the bottom.

4. Trim the excess from the seams, clip corners and turn to the right side. Press. Stuff lightly with cotton batting.

5. For the arms, fold the arms as indicated by the broken line and stitch, leaving the short, straight edge open. Turn right side out and stuff. Use a running stitch to secure in place.

6. For the legs, cut two pieces of fabric 6" x 1 1/4". Fold in the edges and press. Fold each piece in half and stitch. The pieces should now resemble tubes. To form knees, tie a knot in the center of each tube, or leg. Pin the legs to the body at the places indicated on the pattern, and stitch the openings closed using a running stitch.

7. For the ears, stitch the small circles together, leaving an opening through which to turn the fabric right side out. Stuff lightly. Gather slightly at the opening and attach above the arm with a running stitch.

8. Use the large circles to form the feet, following the directions for the ears.

9. Using quilting thread, outline the neck, hands, and muscles with a running stitch, snugging the thread enough to pucker.

Oliver Button Is a Sissy

Tomie dePaola

New York: Harcourt Brace Jovanovich, 1979

and

Now One Foot, Now the Other

Tomie dePaola

New York: G. P. Putnam's Sons, 1981

SUMMARIES

In *Oliver Button Is a Sissy*, a young boy has interests that distinguish him from the other boys, and he faces teasing and rejection until he shows his ability in a talent show. This book is based on dePaola's personal experiences.

In *Now One Foot, Now the Other*, a grandfather teaches his grandson to walk and then, after a stroke, their roles are reversed. This story beautifully illustrates a positive relationship between a child and grandparent.

ACTIVITY

After reading the books and listening to a taped interview with dePaola, children and their parents may discuss the obstacles young children face, such as peer rejection, and the special roles of grandparents in their lives.

 MATERIALS

- Copy of books
- Taped interview with dePaola (available from the Trumpet Club, P.O. Box 604, Holmes, PA, 19043)
- Biographical sketch of the author available from Frank Schaffer Publications
- Storycase container, preferably one that will securely hold the cassette tape. The outside may be illustrated with a photo of dePaola.

 ADDITIONAL NOTES

Tomie dePaola's *Nana Upstairs & Nana Downstairs* (New York: Puffin Books, 1978) may be substituted for either of the books in this storycase.

A storycase may be developed around any author.

Owl Moon

Jane Yolen

New York: Scholastic, 1987

SUMMARY

A child and her father go owling on a clear, bright winter night. The feelings and thoughts that accompany this first-time venture are expressed from the child's point of view. The illustrations further enhance the beauty of this story, which received a Caldecott award in 1988.

ACTIVITY

The child may read the work aloud to his or her family or, using a tape recording, the child may follow along as author Jane Yolen narrates. Parent and child may then enjoy a quiet walk together.

 ## MATERIALS

- Copy of book
- Copy of tape (Scholastic, 1988)
- Storycase container that holds cassette tape securely in place (see illustrations for constructing the *Owl Moon* bag on page 96)

 ## ADDITIONAL NOTES

Publishers' information about the author and illustrator may be included.

Owl Moon

Instructions for making the *Owl Moon* bag

Materials

Blue fabric bag with handles
Dark brown fabric 6" x 8"
Light brown fabric 5 3/4" x 5 1/4"
Yellow or off-white fabric, cut in a 2 1/2" circle
Fabric glue
Brown and yellow fabric markers or paint
Needle and thread of contrasting colors
1" Velcro dot or square

Instructions

1. Using dark brown fabric, fold in 2 corners to form a peak.

2. Glue and stitch in place.

3. Create a pocket by gluing or stitching the light brown fabric to the front of the dark brown.

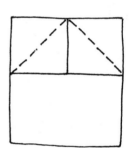

4. Sew the Velcro to the peak.

5. Fold down the peak and mark the light brown fabic for the second Velcro placement. Stitch the second Velcro piece into place.

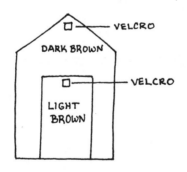

6. Using a marker or paint, add eyes, feathers, and a beak.

7. Glue or stitch pocket to blue bag.

8. Cut a full or half-moon shape from the white or yellow fabric and glue or stitch to bag.

9. Label bag with book title.

From *Storycases: Book Surprises to Take Home.* © 1996. Teacher Ideas Press. 1-800-237-6124.

A Picture for Harold's Room

Crockett Johnson

New York: HarperCollins Children's Books, 1960

SUMMARY

Throughout this book, Harold uses a purple crayon to draw his journey from page to page. His imagination continues and, after realizing how small he is in this big world, he crosses out his picture, then makes a life-size drawing of himself in front of a mirror. Before going to bed, he draws a picture to hang on his wall.

ACTIVITY

Children create "framed" pictures for their rooms or someone else's room.

 ## MATERIALS

- Copy of book
- "Framed" drawing paper, reproduced from the illustration on page 98
- Crayons in a container
- Large envelope to contain all materials

 ## ADDITIONAL NOTES

Label the container of crayons as belonging to the storycase.

A Picture for Harold's Room

Enlarge to 8 1/2" x 11".

From *Storycases: Book Surprises to Take Home.* © 1996. Teacher Ideas Press. 1-800-237-6124.

Polar Bear, Polar Bear, What Do You Hear?

Bill Martin, Jr.

New York: Henry Holt, 1991

SUMMARY

This animal story is a takeoff of Bill Martin, Jr.'s, *Brown Bear, Brown Bear*. In this descriptive story, many new words ending in *ing* are introduced, including *trumpeting*, *yelping*, and *braying*.

ACTIVITY

Children wear headbands picturing the animals and make their sounds in the order they appear in the story. This is effective with a group of children, but an individual child may change headbands as the story progresses, or all members of a family may participate.

 ### MATERIALS

- Copy of book
- Set of headbands to match the animals in the story (see patterns on pages 100–105)
- Paper or fabric shopping bag, picturing a polar bear, to contain all materials

 ### ADDITIONAL NOTES

Children may draw their own animal figures for the headbands or write the animal names on the front of the bands.

Polar Bear, Polar Bear, What Do You Hear?

Headband patterns

Enlarge as desired, color, and attach to headbands.

Polar Bear, Polar Bear, What Do You Hear?

Polar Bear, Polar Bear, What Do You Hear?

Polar Bear, Polar Bear, What Do You Hear?

Polar Bear, Polar Bear, What Do You Hear?

Polar Bear, Polar Bear, What Do You Hear?

The Queen of Hearts

Traditional Rhyme

SUMMARY

See page 107 for a reproducible copy of this traditional rhyme.

ACTIVITY

Child acts out rhyme at home for parents by wearing crown, stealing tarts, and reprimanding the knave. Parents or siblings may be enlisted to play the queen, king, or knave. Parents could use this opportunity to discuss appropriate ways to show anger.

 ### MATERIALS

- Three paper headbands
- Scepter
- Paper plate with paper tarts (see page 108 for heart patterns with which to construct the headbands, scepter, and tarts)
- Laminated copy of poem
- Student-decorated lunch bag to hold all materials

 ### ADDITIONAL NOTES

Children themselves may create this storycase, which they can take home to keep.

The Queen of Hearts

The Queen of Hearts

The Queen of Hearts,
She made some tarts,
All on a summer's day.

The Knave of Hearts,
He stole the tarts
And took them clean away.

The King of Hearts
Called for tarts
And beat the knave full sore;

The Knave of Hearts
Brought back the tarts
And vowed he'd steal no more.

Cut out and laminate rhyme to cardboard. Children who take this storycase home may be given their very own copy of this traditional rhyme.

From *Storycases: Book Surprises to Take Home.* © 1996. Teacher Ideas Press. 1-800-237-6124.

The Queen of Hearts

Patterns for hearts

Make the scepter by attaching the large heart shape to a dowel.

Attach any of the other shapes to headbands and a paper plate to complete the props.

Rain

Robert Kalan

New York: Greenwillow Books, 1991

SUMMARY

The word *rain* is used in a unique way over the deep-colored pages of this book. In addition to the before-and-after effects of rain, the author, with the help of illustrator Donald Crews, uses a minimum of words to explore concepts of color, as well as weather.

ACTIVITY

Children may compare and contrast this book with other books emphasizing the theme of rain, noting format, illustration techniques, storyline, and language.

 ### MATERIALS

- Copy of the book
- One or two additional books, such as *Peter Spier's Rain* by Peter Spier (New York: Doubleday, 1982) and *Rain, Rain* by Joy Cowley (New Zealand: Ready to Read, 1984)
- Storycase container

 ### ADDITIONAL NOTES

Children may write and illustrate a page for a class book entitled *Things to Do on a Rainy Day*, using the reproducible figure on page 110. See page 111 for a pattern with which to make the book's cover.

Rain

Reproducible page for *Things to Do on a Rainy Day*

Punch a hole through the covers (see page 111) and pages and attach together with a plastic or metal ring.

On a rainy day you could:

Rain

Pattern for the front and back covers of *Things to Do on a Rainy Day*

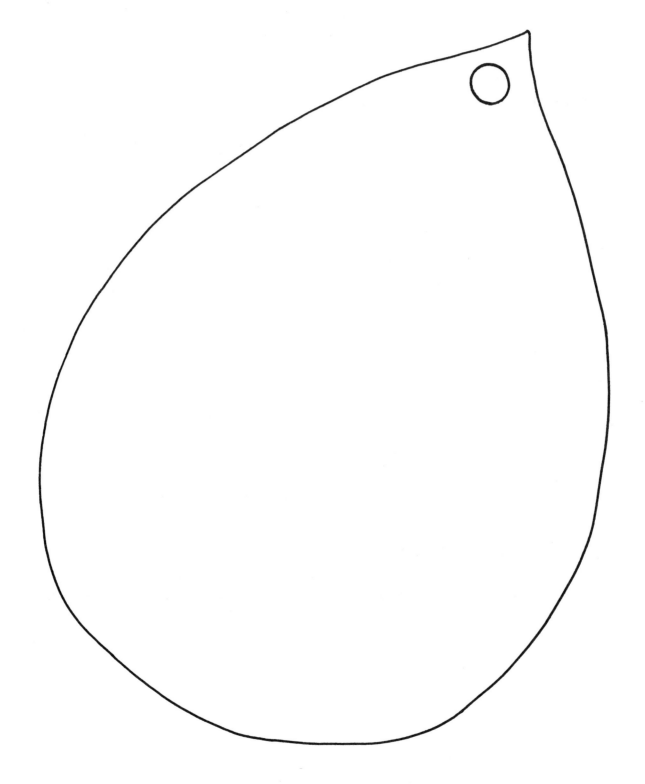

Seven Little Rabbits

John Becker

New York: Scholastic, 1973

SUMMARY

In this repetitive book, seven rabbits walk down the road to visit their friend Toad. One by one, the rabbits get tired and stop to sleep in the mole's hole. The rabbits continue on until the last one falls asleep and dreams of seven little rabbits walking down the road.

ACTIVITY

As the book is read, the child moves toy rabbits along a path, practicing subtraction and the concept of one less. As the story progresses, the rabbits are placed in a hole one by one.

MATERIALS

- Copy of book
- Seven small rabbits made of wood, plastic, or paper
- One mole
- One toad (animal patterns are on page 113)
- Shoebox with hole in lid (see illustration on page 113)
- Path for lid (see pattern on page 114)

ADDITIONAL NOTES

Attach the lid to the box with wide tape after slitting the corners. The lid should open and close as if it is on a hinge. The interior of the box may include stairs and furnishings for mole's house and the tape recording of the book, available from Scholastic.

Seven Little Rabbits

The shoebox will look like this:

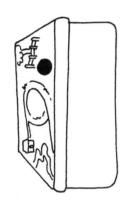

Cut a hole in the lid.

Patterns for the mold, toad, and rabbits

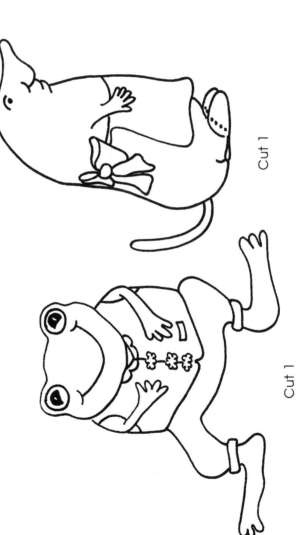

Cut 7

Cut 1

Cut 1

From *Storycases: Book Surprises to Take Home.* © 1996. Teacher Ideas Press. 1-800-237-6124.

Seven Little Rabbits

Pattern for the path on the shoebox lid

Reproduce, color, and glue to lid.

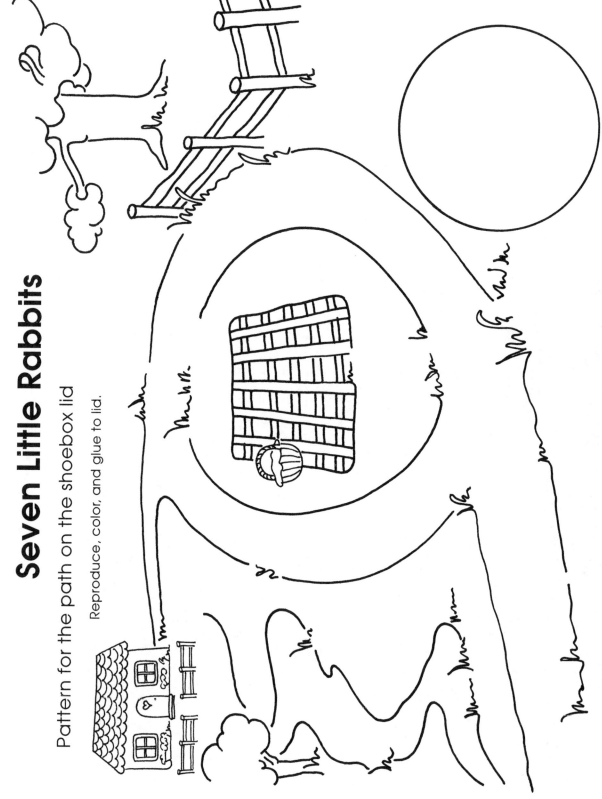

Shoes from Grandpa

Mem Fox

New York: Franklin Watts, 1989

SUMMARY

Based on the style of *The House That Jack Built*, this book tells of a young girl who receives a variety of clothing from her family to go with the shoes that Grandpa gave her. Unfortunately, not all of the clothes match, as shown by the illustrations, and Jessie still wants one specific item—blue jeans.

ACTIVITY

Child dresses up in clothes provided to act out the story.

 MATERIALS

- Copy of book
- Low, red boots
- Reddish-purple socks
- Dark shirt
- Sweater
- Blouse with ribbons and bows
- Coat
- Knitted, striped scarf
- Alligator-type hat
- Bunny-shaped mittens
- Small suitcase to contain all items

 ADDITIONAL NOTES

Similar clothing items for boys may be added or substituted.

Skyfire

Frank Asch

New York: Scholastic, 1984

SUMMARY

Little Bear spots a strange new thing in the sky that he has never seen before. It is a rainbow, but he believes the sky is on fire. As he throws a bucket of water on the rainbow to put the "fire" out, the rainbow fades, convincing him the sky really has been on fire.

ACTIVITY

After reading the story, the child may use a prism to explore the color spectrum and refracted light.

 MATERIALS

- Copy of book
- Prism, with protective container
- Storycase container decorated with rainbows

Ten in a Bed

Penny Dale

Pleasant Hill, CA: Discovery Toys, 1988

SUMMARY

A young child attempts to fall asleep in an over-crowded bed and finds it difficult to roll over. As he does, his stuffed animals fall out one at a time. Alone and lonely in his bed, the child encourages his animals to join him once again.

ACTIVITY

As the story is read, the child recites the part of the little boy as he rolls each animal out of bed: "And the little one said, 'Roll over, roll over'."

 ## MATERIALS

- Copy of book
- Cardboard bed made from a small box
- Ten "animals" made by gluing wiggly or felt eyes to pom-poms
- Pillowcase or overnight bag to contain all materials

 ## ADDITIONAL NOTES

Five Little Ducks by Raffi (New York: Crown Books, 1992) and *Seven Little Rabbits* by John Becker (New York: Scholastic, 1973) may be adapted to this storycase.

The Three Bears

Paul Galdone

New York: Clarion Books, 1985

SUMMARY

In this traditional tale, a little girl visits the home of three bears while they are out for a walk. After tasting their porridge and sampling their chairs and beds, Goldilocks falls asleep in Little Bear's bed, where the bears discover her upon their return.

ACTIVITY

After reading the story with parents, the child may play "The Three Bears Alphabet Walk," which provides an opportunity for practicing letter recognition.

MATERIALS

- Copy of book
- "The Three Bears Alphabet Walk" (see reproducible game board illustration on page 119)
- Dice and three plastic bears or other game pieces
- Expandable envelope to contain all materials

ADDITIONAL NOTES

Any commercially available figures of Goldilocks and the Three Bears may be included to help retell the story.

Bear-shaped sponges may be included for sponge paintings.

The Three Bears

Reproduce, mount on cardboard, and laminate the illustration below.

THE THREE BEARS ALPHABET WALK

Roll the dice and move the number of spaces indicated. Name the letter. Players who cannot name the letter should be assisted by the other players.

Three Little Kittens

Paul Galdone

New York: Clarion Books, 1988

SUMMARY

The Three Little Kittens lose their mittens and report the loss to Mother Cat, who scolds them. When they locate the missing mittens, the kittens are rewarded with pie, which they eat with their mittens on. When the mittens become soiled, the kittens are forced to wash them. The modern illustrations of this version resemble children's homes of today.

ACTIVITY

After reading the story, the child, with parental assistance, makes muffin pies. In imitation of the events in the story, the child may try eating the pie with mittens on, washing the mittens, and hanging them on the clothesline to dry.

 ### MATERIALS

- Copy of book
- One pair of mittens
- Three feet of clothesline
- Two clothespins
- Recipe for muffin pies (see recipe card on page 121)
- Small lunchbox to contain all materials

 ### ADDITIONAL NOTES

Illustrations of Mother Cat and the three kittens, either drawn by the children or taken from a coloring book, may be cut out and mounted on tongue depressors to be used in acting out the story.

Three Little Kittens

Recipe card for muffin pies

Cut out and laminate recipe card. Each child who takes this storycase home may be presented with his or her own copy of this recipe.

Recipe from the classroom of: _____

THREE INDIVIDUAL MUFFIN PIES

6 graham crackers
1/4 cup melted butter
pudding or fruit pie filling

1 tablespoon sugar
3 foil muffin or custard cups

Crush graham crackers, add sugar and butter, and mix thoroughly. Press crumb mixture into muffin cups and fill with pudding or fruit pie filling.

ENJOY!!

From *Storycases: Book Surprises to Take Home.* © 1996. Teacher Ideas Press. 1-800-237-6124.

Three Little Pigs

Traditional Tale

SUMMARY

The Three Little Pigs leave home to start life on their own. In building their homes, they each try a different type of building material—straw, sticks, or bricks.

The first two pigs have their homes blown away by the Big Bad Wolf, from whom they escape to their brother's brick house. Although the wolf tries, he fails to blow down the brick house. The ending of the tale will vary depending on the version used.

ACTIVITY

The child moves magnetic figures of the animals from house to house in telling the story or acting it out as the story is read.

 MATERIALS

- Copy of book
- Round metal tin, such as a cookie tin, with the three houses taped or glued to the sides.
- Three paper or wooden pigs, numbered on the front and to which magnets have been attached on the back
- One paper or wooden wolf with a magnet on the back (patterns for the animals and houses are on page 123)
- Storycase container, such as the tin itself, or a larger container, as needed to accommodate the book

Three Little Pigs

Patterns for the wolf, the pigs, and their houses

Cut 3

Cut 1

Cut 3

Time for Bed

Mem Fox

New York: Harcourt Brace Jovanovich, 1993

SUMMARY

This beautifully illustrated bedtime book establishes a repetitive pattern as each adult and young child is told that it is time for bed. At the conclusion of the book, there is a picture of a child being put into bed. This is a great book to be read every evening, as the predictable verse helps to lull a young child to sleep.

ACTIVITY

The parents read the book to their children in bed, having surrounded them with stuffed animals like the ones mentioned in the book.

 ### MATERIALS

- Copy of book
- Stuffed animals mentioned in text
- Drawstring bag, made from flannel or fabric and having a bedtime theme, to contain all materials

 ### ADDITIONAL NOTES

This storycase may be created in the home by parents and children to be used as a family bedtime ritual. Use any cloth bag as the storycase container and include such things as a favorite bedtime story, pajamas, toothbrush, and a favorite stuffed animal.

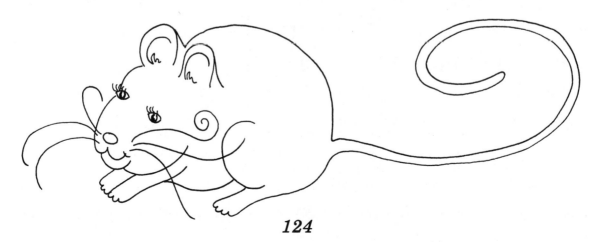

The Truck Book

Harry McNaught
New York: Random House, 1978

SUMMARY

A large variety of trucks and their functions are described with colorful illustrations and easy-to-read text.

ACTIVITY

Child matches the contents of the book with word cards bearing the names of items that trucks carry.

MATERIALS

- Copy of book
- Word cards naming items carried by trucks
- Reusable storage bag or envelope

ADDITIONAL NOTES

Truck: Big Book Edition by Donald Crews (New York: Morrow, 1993) or *Cars and Things That Go* by Richard Scarry (New York: Golden Books, 1974) may be substituted.

This storycase activity is appropriate for any theme or subject.

The Truck Book

Title card for word cards

Reproduce the figure below to make cards on which to write freight items. Trim cards to the 2"-x-6" size indicated and secure together on a ring.

Uncle Vova's Tree

Patricia Polacco

New York: Philomel, 1989

SUMMARY

This is a family story emphasizing the close ties of the extended family and the importance of tradition in a person's life. Uncle Vova shares with the children some of the traditions celebrated by Russian culture and asks the children to remember to carry on the traditions when he is no longer with them.

ACTIVITY

After reading the story together, parents and children may make star ornaments to hang on their Christmas tree or other holiday focal point. Parents can then tell or write about a family tradition celebrated in their home.

 ## MATERIALS

- Copy of book
- Directions for making star ornaments (reproducible instructions are on page 128)
- Reusable storage bag to contain all items

 ## ADDITIONAL NOTES

This storycase may include a class book to which families may contribute stories about their family traditions. Include blank pages for new contributions.

Uncle Vova's Tree

Directions for making a star ornament

Cut a star shape from oak tag or heavy paper using the pattern below.

Decorate with glue and glitter. Tape the star to a dowel or Popsicle stick.

Cut three to four 10" streamers from multicolored crepe paper and attach to the dowel.

Pattern for star shape

The Very Hungry Caterpillar

Eric Carle

New York: Scholastic, 1987

SUMMARY

On Sunday a very hungry caterpillar emerges. As the week progresses he searches for food and eats his way through increasing quantities of "people food," including apples, a pickle, and a cupcake. The caterpillar's life cycle is demonstrated as he builds his cocoon and emerges as a butterfly.

ACTIVITY

As the book is read, the children can slip the foods mentioned over their wrists, which are covered with a caterpillar sock. At the end, a colorful butterfly is revealed from the cocoon container.

 ### MATERIALS

- Copy of book
- Sock and cocoon to represent caterpillar (see cocoon pattern on page 130)
- Scrap felt for caterpillar eyes
- Tag board or paper for making foods (see patterns on pages 131–146)
- Tissue or colorful paper for butterfly (see butterfly pattern on page 148)
- "Cocoon" made from a brown fabric sack or paper envelope to contain all materials

 ### ADDITIONAL NOTES

This storycase may be adapted to *The Little Green Caterpillar* by Yvonne Hooker (New York: Grossett & Dunlap, 1981).

The Very Hungry Caterpillar

COCOON
Cut 1

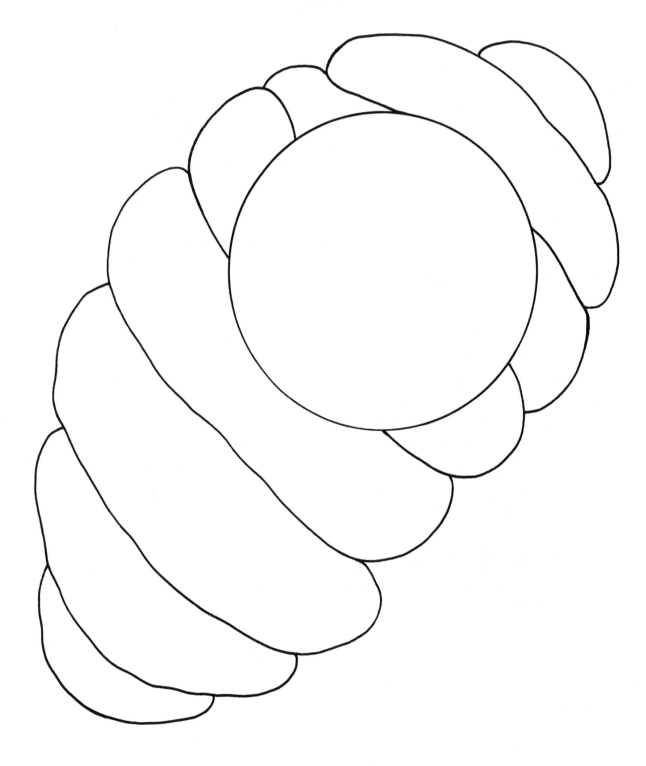

The Very Hungry Caterpillar

APPLE
Cut 1

The Very Hungry Caterpillar

PEAR
Cut 2

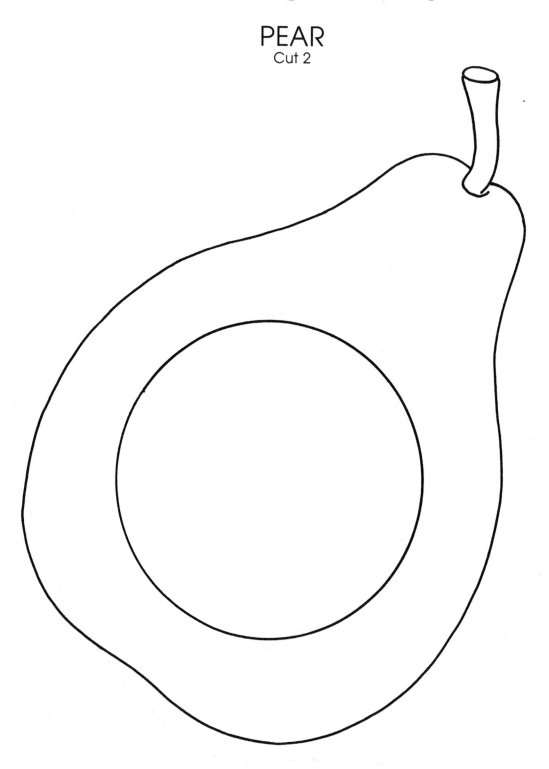

The Very Hungry Caterpillar

PLUM
Cut 3

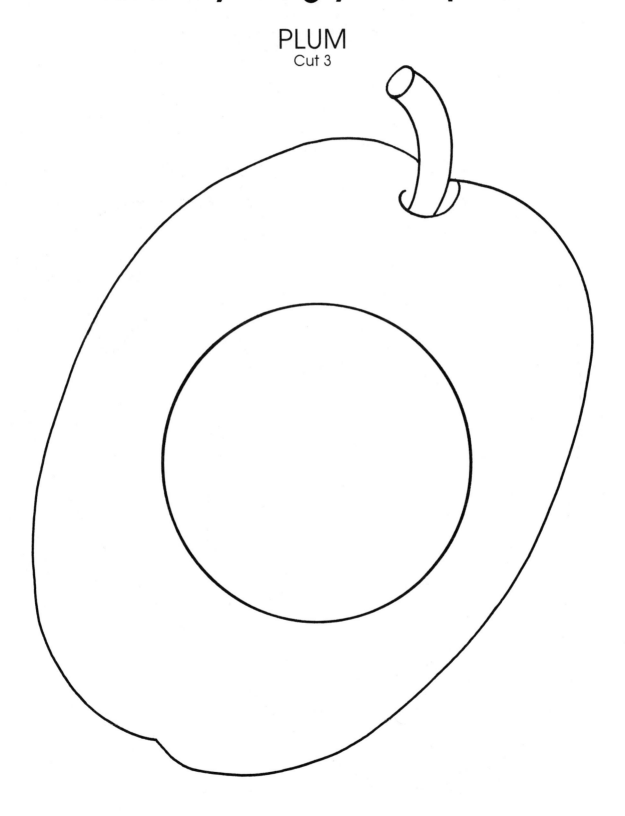

The Very Hungry Caterpillar

STRAWBERRY
Cut 4

The Very Hungry Caterpillar

ORANGE
Cut 5

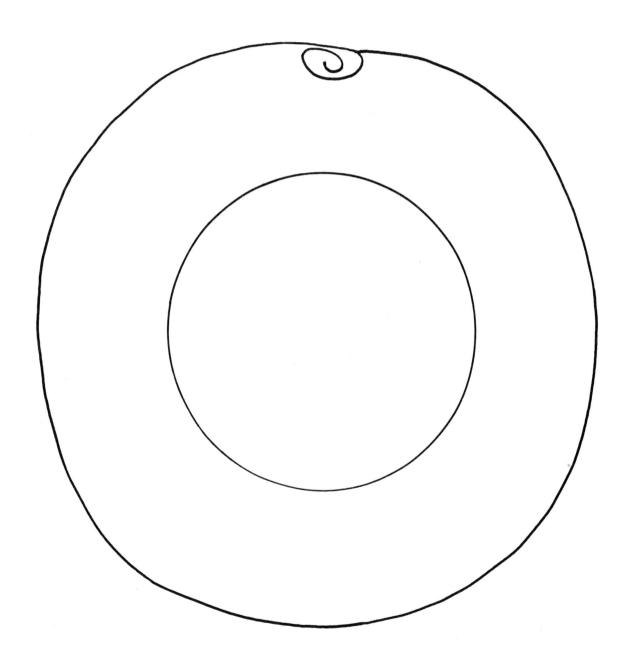

The Very Hungry Caterpillar

PICKLE
Cut 1

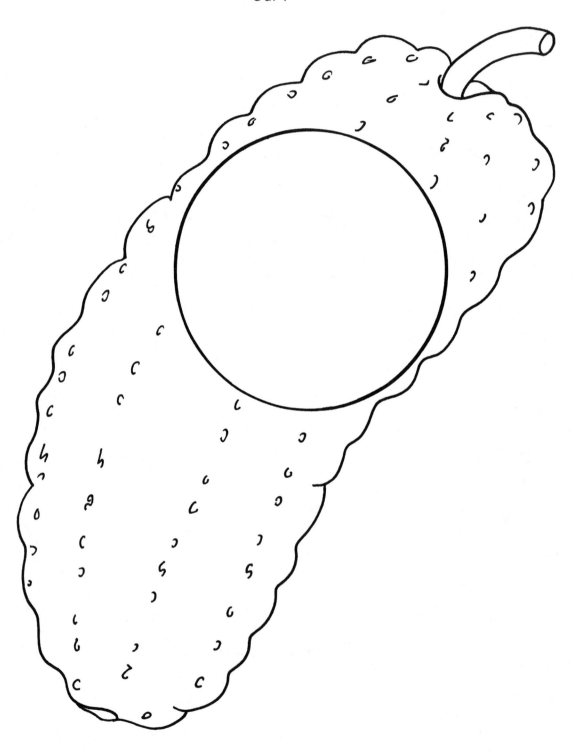

The Very Hungry Caterpillar

SALAMI
Cut 1

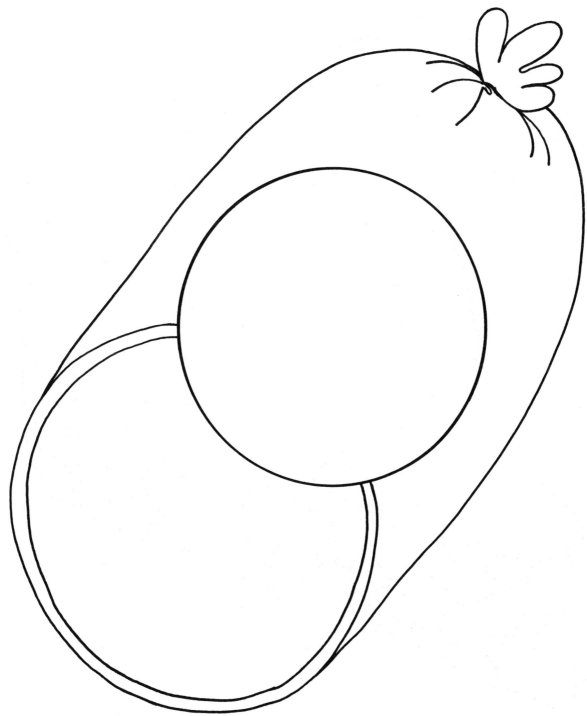

The Very Hungry Caterpillar

CHERRY PIE
Cut 1

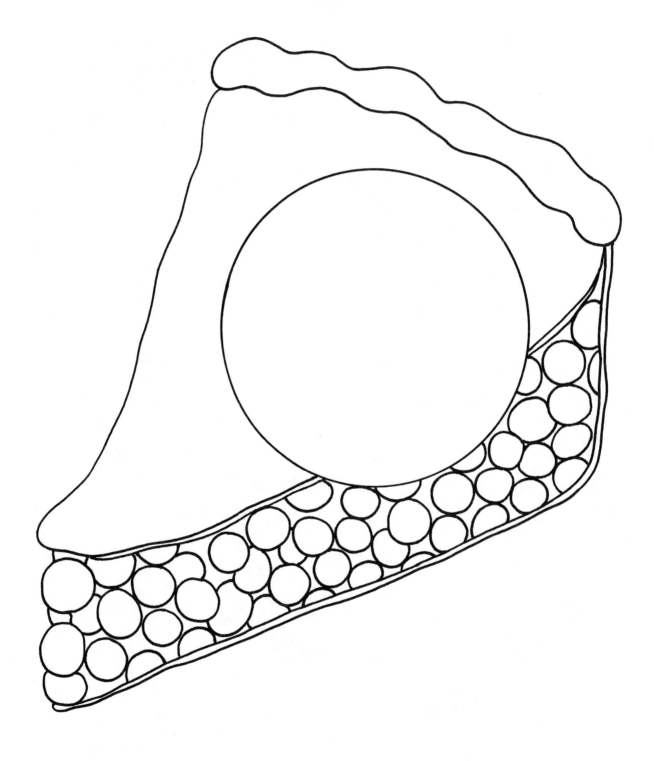

The Very Hungry Caterpillar

WATERMELON
Cut 1

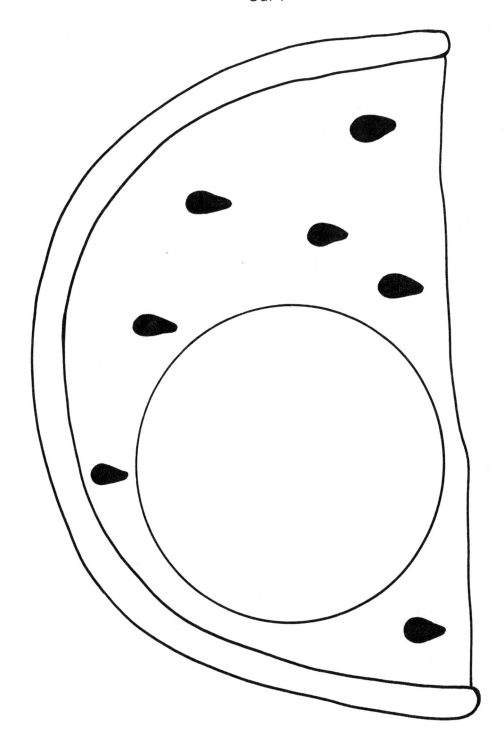

The Very Hungry Caterpillar

CUPCAKE
Cut 1

The Very Hungry Caterpillar

SWISS CHEESE
Cut 1

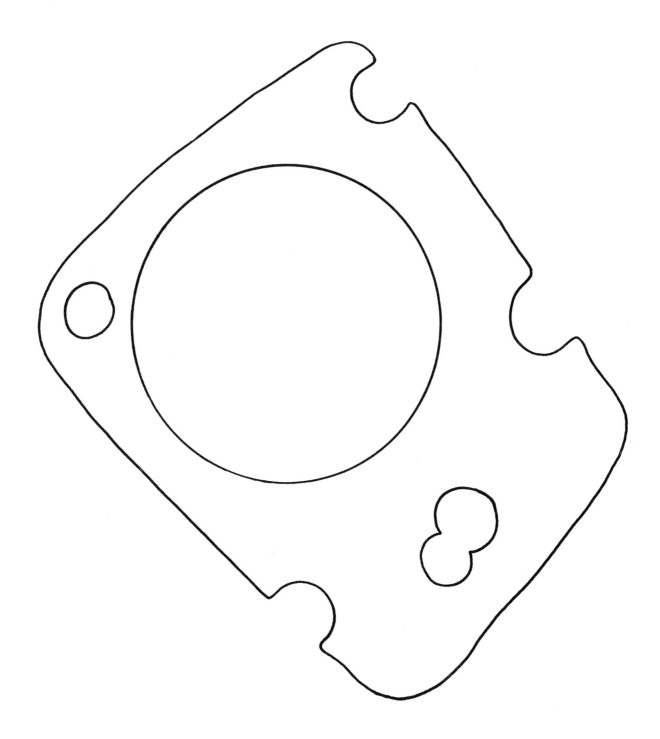

The Very Hungry Caterpillar

SAUSAGE
Cut 1

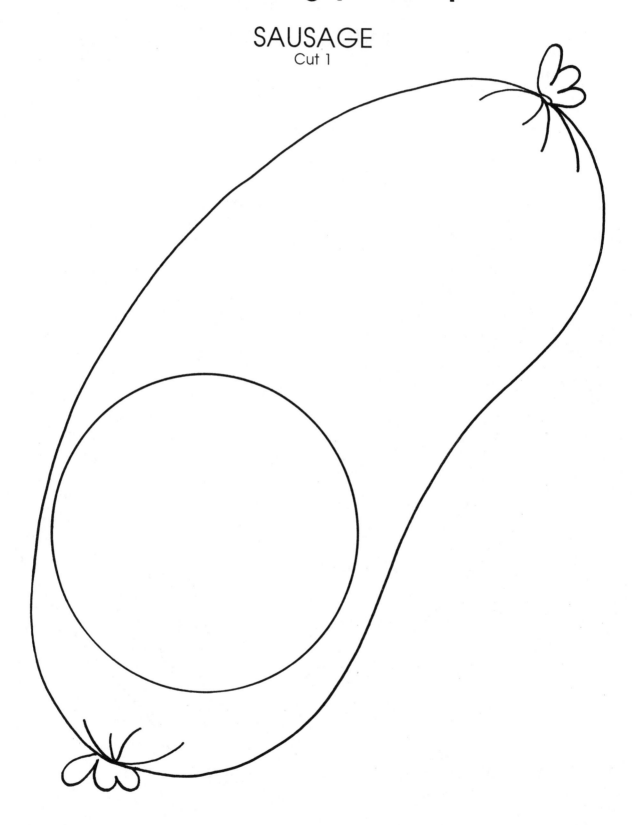

The Very Hungry Caterpillar

LOLLIPOP
Cut 1

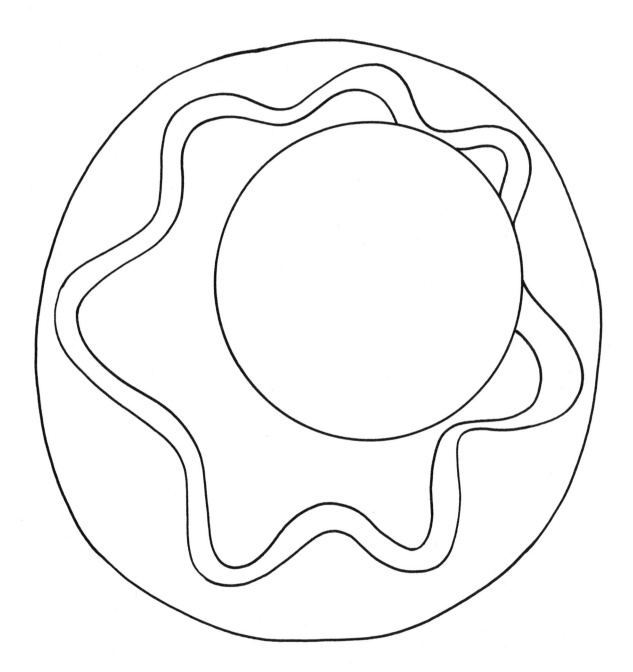

Attach to a Popsicle stick, pencil, or dowel.

The Very Hungry Caterpillar

LEAF
Cut 1

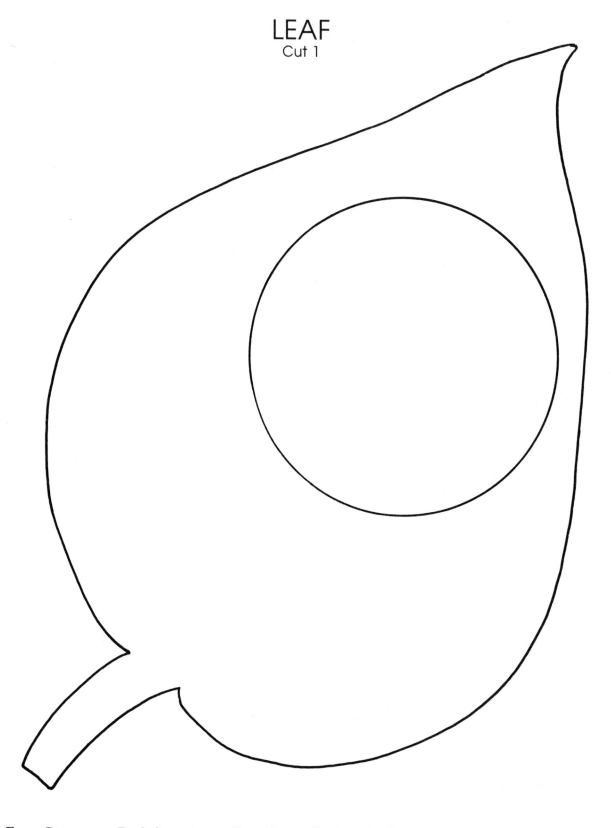

The Very Hungry Caterpillar

ICE CREAM CONE
Cut 1

The Very Hungry Caterpillar

CHOCOLATE CAKE
Cut 1

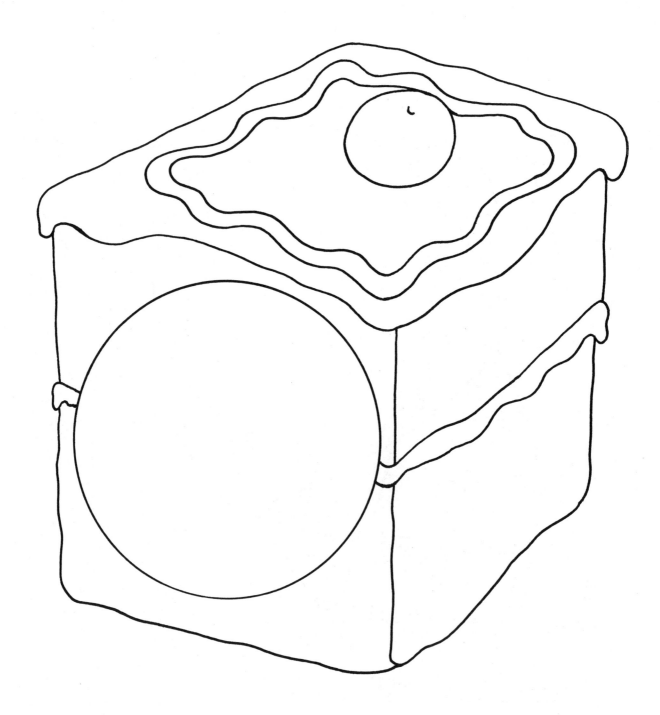

The Very Hungry Caterpillar

SUN
NO HOLE!

The Very Hungry Caterpillar

BUTTERFLY
NO HOLE!

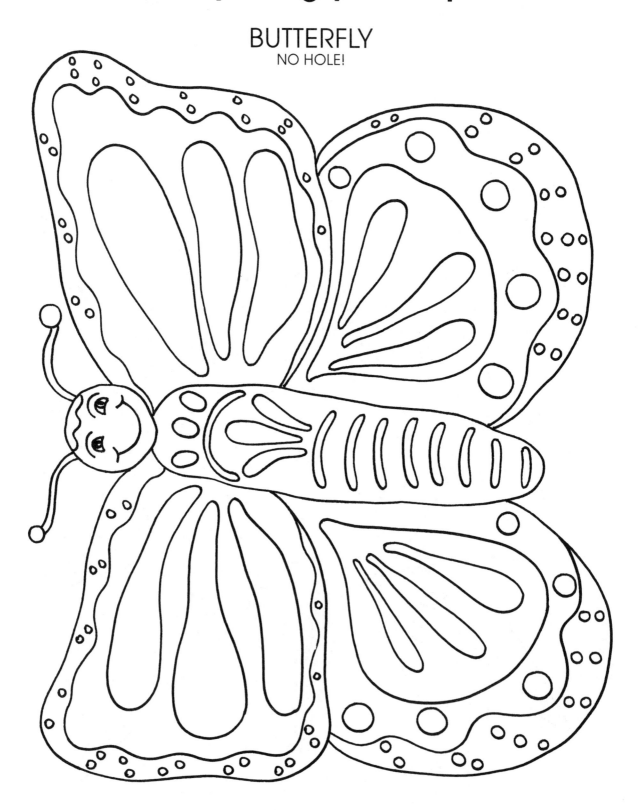

A Visit to Washington, D.C.

Jill Krementz

New York: Scholastic, 1987

SUMMARY

A six-year-old boy takes the reader on a photographic tour of Washington, D.C., telling about each place visited as a child would view it. Factual, supplementary information, which may be of interest, also is given.

ACTIVITY

The child may locate places pictured in the text on a map of Washington, D.C.

MATERIALS

- Copy of book
- Map of Washington, D.C. (two maps of varying detail may be included)
- Pocket folder for book and maps, the outside of which is decorated with a camera or a scene of Washington, D.C., to contain all materials

ADDITIONAL NOTES

A travel journal may be included for use by children who are traveling.

This storycase also may include *Rand McNally's Kids U.S. Road Atlas* (Skokie, IL: Rand McNally, 1992).

We Like Bugs!

Joelene Griffith

East Wenatchee, WA: Learning Workshop, 1993

SUMMARY

The text comprises a catchy song sung by frogs about the insects they like to eat. The different descriptive words and repetitive chorus, along with the Latin rhythm, are especially attractive to children. The "slinky centipede" appears in each verse of the song.

ACTIVITY

The child uses the Slinky Centipede Memory Game to relate the insects to the song. A tape of the song may be listened to as a sing-along.

 MATERIALS

- Copy of book
- Copy of song on cassette tape
- Memory game (see pages 151 and 152)
- Container for game parts such as a reusable storage bag
- Drawstring bag to contain all materials

 ADDITIONAL NOTES

This song is available in Big Book format for classroom use. When appropriate or available, a hand-held tape player with ear phones may be included in the storycase.

We Like Bugs!

Slinky Centipede Memory Game

Shuffle the bug cards and place face down on the floor or table. The children may want to place them in straight rows to help them remember the location. The object of the game is to find matching pairs. A child will turn over two cards; if they match, he or she keeps them. This child continues to play until two are turned over that do not match. If a child turns over the card with the centipede, he or she must mix all the other cards up and then turn over two more cards to see if they match. The game continues until all the bugs are gone except the slinky centipede.

Moth

Moth

Ladybug

Ladybug

Honey Bee

Honey Bee

We Like Bugs!

King Termite

King Termite

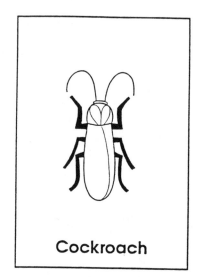

Cockroach

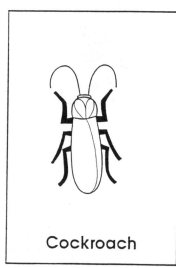

Cockroach

Black Fly

Black Fly

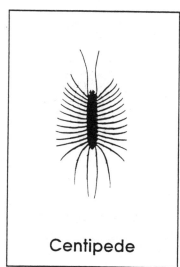

Centipede

Worker Ant

Worker Ant

Wonders of the Sea

Louis Sabin
Mahwah, NJ: Troll, 1982

SUMMARY

This book offers an excellent opportunity for a parent and child to explore the many wonderful things found on the beach and under the sea.

ACTIVITY

Children examine the items from the sea as the book is read to them. They then may categorize them by shape or size.

 ### MATERIALS

- Copy of book
- Collection of seashells and other items from the sea in a reusable storage bag. Sand also may be included.
- Plastic beach bag to hold all materials

 ### ADDITIONAL NOTES

Other appropriate books include *A House for Hermit Crab* by Eric Carle (New York: Picture Book Studio, 1991), *Stina* by Lena Anderson (New York: Greenwillow Books, 1989), and *Swimmy* by Leo Lionni (New York: Knopf Books for Young Readers, 1987).

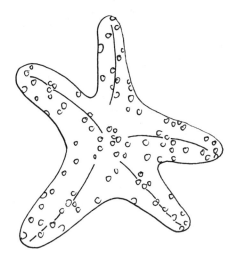

Appendix:
Sources of Materials
and Ideas

LITERATURE-RELATED MATERIALS

Demco
P.O. Box 7488
Madison, WI 53791-9955
1-800-356-1200
Puppets and items related to specific
    books and author-related items

T. S. Denison and Co.
960 Newton Avenue South
Minneapolis, MN 55431
Activity books such as *Cooking Up a
    Story*, *Finger Puppets and Story
    Telling*, *Story Telling with the
    Flannel Board*

Education Center
1607 Battleground Avenue
P.O. Box 9753
Greensboro, NC 27499-0123
1-800-334-0298
Publications with literature-related
    activities; materials for preparing
    activities

Evan-Moor
18 Lower Ratsdale Drive
Monterey, CA 93940
1-800-777-4362
Books of literature-related activities
    and reproducibles such as
    *Headbands for Quick and Easy
    Play Activities*

Folkmanis
1219 Park Avenue
Emeryville, CA 94608
1-510-658-7677
Animal puppets of excellent quality and
    variety

Gaylord Brothers
Box 4901
Syracuse, NY 13221-4901
1-800-448-6160
Bags for books and library-related
    supplies

Gryphon House
P.O. Box 207
Beltsville, MD 20704-0207
Literature activity books such as
    Story Stretchers

The Learning Workshop
132 Eastmont Avenue
East Wenatchee, WA 98802
1-800-752-0663
Thematic interactive units with tapes
    and reproducible materials

Frank Schaffer Publications
23740 Hawthorne Boulevard
Torrance, CA 90505
1-800-421-5565
Literature-related activities, such as
    Literature Notes, and author
    pictures and profiles

Teacher Ideas Press
P.O. Box 6633
Englewood, CO 80155-6633
1-800-237-6124
Books related to literature across the
curriculum, such as *Starting with
Books: An Activities Approach to
Children's Literature, Literature on
the Move: Making and Using Pop-
Up and Lift-Flap Books,* and *An
Author a Month*

BOOK CLUBS

Scholastic Book Clubs
P.O. Box 7502
Jefferson City, MO 65102

Troll Book Clubs
320 Route 17
Mahwah, NJ 07430

Trumpet Book Clubs
Dell Publishing Co.
1 Dag Hammarskjold Plaza
New York, NY 10017

Weekly Reader Corporation
3000 Cindel Drive
P.O. Box 8037
Delran, NJ 08075

INDEX